Introducing Children's Literature

Introducing Children's Literature is an ideal guide to reading children's literature through the perspective of literary history. Focusing on the literary movements from Romanticism to Postmodernism, Thacker and Webb examine the concerns of each period and the ways in which these concerns influence and are influenced by the children's literature of the time.

Each section begins with a general chapter, which explains the relationship between the major concerns of each literary period and the formal and thematic qualities of children's texts. Close readings of selected texts follow to demonstrate the key defining characteristics of the form of writing and the literary movements.

This is the first text to set children's literature within a relationship to writing for adults and is essential reading for students studying writing for children.

Books discussed include: *Little Women*, *The Water-Babies*, *Alice in Wonderland*, *The Wonderful Wizard of Oz*, *The Secret Garden*, *Mary Poppins*, *Charlotte's Web* and *Clockwork*.

Deborah Cogan Thacker is Field Chair for English Literature at the University of Gloucestershire.

Jean Webb is Director of the International Centre for Research in Primary English and Children's Literature and Senior Lecturer in English Studies at University College Worcester.

Introducing Children's Literature

From Romanticism to Postmodernism

Deborah Cogan Thacker
and
Jean Webb

Routledge
Taylor & Francis Group

LONDON AND NEW YORK

First published 2002
by Routledge
2 Park Square, Milton Park, Abingdon, Oxon OX14 4RN

Simultaneously published in the USA and Canada
by Routledge
711 Third Ave, New York, NY 10017

Reprinted 2005

Routledge is an imprint of the Taylor & Francis Group

© 2002 Deborah Cogan Thacker and Jean Webb

Typeset in Garamond by
Florence Production Ltd, Stoodleigh, Devon.

British Library Cataloguing in Publication Data
A catalogue record for this book is available
from the British Library

Library of Congress Cataloging in Publication Data
A catalog record for this book has been requested

ISBN 0 415 20410 0 (hbk)
ISBN 0 415 20411 9 (pbk)

Contents

SECTION FIVE
Postmodernism

This book is dedicated to the memory of
my father, Edward J. Cogan

Preface

This book suggests ways of reading children's literature within the context of literary history. The authors provide a broad overview of the influence of literary 'movements', such as Romanticism, Modernism and Postmodernism, on the production of children's literature, and argue for the relevance of such texts to the study of mainstream literary history. The general discussions are accompanied by a series of short essays about individual children's books. The readings offered in these short chapters suggest ways of applying the broader framework of literary history to particular texts, and are not intended to provide definitive (if there can ever be such a thing) analyses of the chosen texts.

While the authors intend to offer a new way of thinking about children's literature in relation to a more inclusive sense of literary history, this book is neither a 'rewriting' of either the history of children's literature, nor a revisionist challenge to the literary histories which already exist. It is selective rather than comprehensive, and exclusively Anglo-American in focus. There are a number of literary histories available (see the Bibliography, p. 165), which provide more detailed accounts of children's books in an historical context. Rather than duplicate this material, this book offers a new way of shaping it, with the intention of reading children's literature *through* familiar ways of looking at mainstream literature. By providing this perspective on children's literature, we have chosen to emphasise narrative texts and to concentrate on those works of fiction which are continually published and republished, rather than 'popular' fiction, series books or the wide variety of books produced as part of the children's publishing market. There are, admittedly, many other books to consider, and it is hoped that the ways of approaching texts suggested here will lead readers to find equally relevant examples.

At a time when the Anglo-American focus on the study of children's literature is being challenged, it may seem retrograde to ignore the richness of international children's literature. Postcolonial approaches to literature have important relevance to what can be said about the literature that is produced for children, and children's literature in English can also be implicated as a colonialising force throughout the world. It is not the intention of the authors to add to this pressure, and there is no claim for the superiority of the texts discussed. The influence of literary movements remains the primary focus of this text, and the predominance of specifically Western, and frequently, Anglo-American, concerns must be acknowledged. It is hoped that the perspectives offered here will lead others to investigate more fully, and more inclusively, specific texts and specific histories.

This book, therefore, does not offer a radical reworking of the definitions of children's literature, nor does it seek to provide a singular theoretical framework within which to consider its chosen texts. What it does do, however, is to suggest a new way of understanding the importance of children's literature as a part of literary production as a whole, rather than as merely a specialised area of study.

Acknowledgements

This book is based on a series of lectures originally delivered as part of an undergraduate course in Children's Literature in 1994. The material has been adapted to reflect the transformation that the subject has undergone since that time.

The authors wish to acknowledge the academics, researchers and students who have contributed to the development of the subject and those who have discussed, in formal and less formal ways, the readings presented here.

It would be impossible to list all those whose conversations, debates and writing have been influential to the focus of this book, but we would like to mention the members of the British Association for Lecturers in Children's Literature. Although this organisation is awaiting a new direction, the twice-annual meetings with, among many others, Professor Kimberley Reynolds, Dr Christine Wilkie, Dr David Rudd and Aidan and Nancy Chambers helped to reinforce our sense that children's literature is an exciting, innovative and challenging field. The work of Lissa Paul, Jack Zipes, Rod McGillis, Perry Nodelman and John Stephens has also been similarly inspiring.

A special acknowledgement must, however, go to Professor Peter Hunt, whose unstinting encouragement and support during the gestation of this work and, indeed, throughout the course of our research, has been both challenging and enlightening.

Dr Jean Webb would like to acknowledge, in particular, the support of the English Department at University College, Worcester for time to carry out work on this book, and the International Youth Library in Munich for a research fellowship and the use of their resources. She would also like to thank Anna Heidapalsdottir, Debbie Sly, Jill Terry and Vivienne Smith (and the tolerance of her dog, Henry).

Dr Deborah Thacker would like to acknowledge the support and encouragement of her colleagues in the School of English at the University of Gloucestershire and to thank them for granting her a period of research leave to begin the book. Thanks, too, go to Ben, Duncan and Sam for letting her read to them and to Kevin, for telling her to keep on going.

Introduction

The purpose of this book is to provide a very particular context for understanding the developments and shifting concerns of children's literature throughout its history. While children's texts will be considered within an historical context, the focus of this study will also consider the extent to which some children's texts contain an awareness of the implications of writing for children. Such a focus embraces a range of definitions of 'authorship', 'reading', 'the child' and 'the literary', which can be best understood by relating children's literature to a wider understanding of literary history as a whole.

There have already been a number of 'histories' of children's literature, notably Townsend's *Written for Children* (1976) and, more recently, Hunt's *Introduction to Children's Literature* (1994) and *Children's Literature, An Illustrated History* (1995), and this book is intended to complement these, rather than to offer another version of them. While such histories give a shape to the wide range of works available to children, and provide useful contextual information for those studying children's literature, their specialist focus reinforces the separateness of the texts considered from any notion of literary history as a whole. This will not, therefore, be an account of the wide range of children's books on offer, nor will it provide lists of texts according to the historical period in which they were first published. There is already a large area of scholarship devoted to investigating the roots of this prolific area of literary production, and many scholars provide critical readings of children's texts within an historical context. Again, the discussion in the pages that follow is intended to acknowledge the importance of that work and to frame the observations made in previous scholarship in order to relate children's literature to a wider understanding of literary history.

Critical investigations of children's literature frequently embrace an historical context and acknowledge the importance of the changing concerns within the texts over time. However, while works examining the influence of historical events and trends on the books themselves are increasingly available, it is very rare to see a mention of a children's book in investigations of literary history in general. In terms of providing an understanding of the ways in which these changing concerns are interdependent, the implication that children's literature can be separated from mainstream concerns undermines the importance of these texts and their place within literary history.

While there are exceptions, such as Juliet Dusinberre's valuable investigation of modernism, *Alice to the Lighthouse: Children's Books and Radical Experiments in Art* (1999), for the most part, children's books are largely ignored in this branch of literary scholarship. It may be that mainstream literary historians assume that books written for children are independent of the forces that influence literary change. Alternatively, the texts themselves, focused as they are on educational values, may appear merely to be exercises in social control. Children's literature specialists have demonstrated repeatedly that the exclusion of such texts belies the complexity of their engagement with literary questions, whether thematic or formal.

This volume seeks to address this exclusion, and to suggest that texts written either directly or indirectly for a young audience contribute significantly to an understanding of literary movements, which reflect the history of, in this case, the Anglo-American literary tradition. If one traces the development of literature in the last two centuries and engages with shifts in aesthetic concerns, from Romanticism to Modernism and Postmodernism, it is possible to see the relevance of children's literature to a map of literature as a whole. Rather than merely tracing a chronological route, the emphasis on a body of concerns defined by these 'movements' within literary history demonstrates the ways in which books written for children embrace the aesthetic of any particular age, but often anticipate, and perhaps inspire, innovation.

This study will not, therefore, be exhaustive. The emphasis will be on the study of those texts which are, for the most part, recognised as enduring. Among the many thousands of books published for children, few engage in powerful ways with notions of authorship and aesthetic concerns. Each critic's definition of 'enduring' qualities will differ, and there will be many who might challenge the implication of exceptionalism implied by the 'value' attributed to the texts discussed in this book. While the expansion of children's literature publishing since the mid-nineteenth century and the diverse range of texts available will be discussed, it is those texts which exhibit a self-consciousness about the task of writing for children that will be the main object for exploration. These may not necessarily be the books that are most frequently read by children, but they are certainly the texts which are most *about* writing for children and thus demonstrate the shifting of the author/reader relationship throughout the last two centuries. These are the texts that explore the task of writing for children, rather than repeat tried and tested formulae.

A definition of literary history as a means of exploring the ways in which literature articulates the relationship between the individual and society cannot ignore the literature written for children. While a few key texts find their way into mainstream studies of the history of literature (Carroll's two 'Alice' books are the best example), most are invisible to literary historians. The lack of acknowledgement of the influence of children's books on our changing perceptions of the relationship between the author and the reader, or the place of the 'value' of the 'literary' must be addressed. Therefore, this volume intends to consider the implications of this isolation of children's texts from an understanding of literary history as a whole.

While it may be less surprising that the content of children's literature responds to historical change and world events, a critical study such as this reveals the extent to which the relationship between the adult author and the child as reader is influenced by shifting aesthetic concerns. This book suggests a way of studying children's literature through an understanding of the way such shifts are articulated through a dialogue between author and reader, as in any literary text.

Although it is our intention to emphasise the commonality between the ideas expressed in children's fiction and other literary texts, it is also the purpose of this book to demonstrate the extent to which children's literature must also always be a special case. While all literature is based on a power relationship, and all is dependent on a shared understanding of language, children's literature is based on a relationship that is less equal than that between adult reader and adult author. One of the purposes of reading, and of stories, for children, is to admit them into an adult language system and, thus, one of the defining features of children's books is the tendency of the voice of the narrator to acknowledge the reader's 'apprenticeship' to the written word.

Children's literature knowingly engages with the idea of power at the heart of the relationship between author and reader, from its roots in the radical shifting of aesthetic ideas that are defined under the broad term, Romanticism. Its existence originally arose from a growing interest in childhood as 'innocence' and thus a revelation of the 'true nature' of self, rather than as a time to control the inborn sinfulness of mankind. A conception of the author/artist as a possessor of particular kinds of superior knowledge and the valorisation of the power of the imagination suggests that writing for children provides valuable insights into the changing conception of authorship. By tracing the development of children's literature from within an understanding of the shifting concerns of literature as a whole, it is possible to see the connection between the shifting power relationship of author and reader of any text. The degree of 'authority' with which authors of children's books provided fictional worlds for their readers can, thus, be seen to change in response to historical and cultural change. Beginning from a position of confidence in the purpose of children's literature to address the underlying 'deep real self' suggested by Coleridge, it is possible to perceive a growing discomfort in the relationship between author and reader over time. Though such a shift can be defined in terms of Western culture's changing definition of childhood and the world events which shape individual experience, it is also indelibly linked to the confidence of authors about their ability to offer possible worlds to any readership.

This emphasis on the ways in which the relationship between author and reader change throughout time also has implications for the part which children's literature plays in each individual's reading history. The reading experiences encountered in childhood define the relationship between the teller and the told, and thus play a formative role in the construction of readers (Meek, 1988). Early relationships with fiction offer expectations about the possible relationships between the teller and the told. Although the texts may imply an apprentice readership, the narrative relationships set up by such early experiences are not, however, simple. Many of the books discussed here provide challenging models for young readers, though vocabulary and subject matter might be more 'child-orientated'.

Although this will not be the primary focus of this study, the continuity implied by the formative function of children's literature must be acknowledged. Some of the readers of children's books at one particular time will become authors in another. Dusinberre's conviction, that Modernist art arose in part as a response to the children's fantasies read by Modernist writers in their childhoods, is a tantalising one, and deserves further exploration (Dusinberre 1999).

The Romantic aesthetic provides a central core of ideas about both childhood and authorship which are inflected by subsequent literary and historical movements. Thus, the authoritarianism of the Victorian expansion of the literary domain, the disruptions of the *fin de siècle* and, finally, the search for the new and the alienation that defines Modernism and Postmodernism, can all be seen as reflections of, and responses to, this aesthetic. Viewed in this way, the project of writing for children becomes a complex and ambiguous pursuit, one that articulates the changing nature of authorship in the face of social change.

At the same time, the growing separation of children's literature from the literary mainstream becomes more evident in terms of production and public status, so the ideas and stylistic innovations which mark each period converge. It is hoped that the demonstration of this convergence will provide many opportunities for exploring the complexity of children's texts in relation to their mainstream contemporaries and enrich the possibilities of dialogue between the two critical traditions.

Studying children's literature in this way is made possible by the engagement of a wide variety of theoretical perspectives, and the move away from a 'canonical' approach to literature in general. The emphasis, in the last few decades, on the cultural context of literary production, on the gendering of language, for instance, and on the importance of the reader in the making of meaning, has meant a wide diversification of critical approaches to texts written expressly for children. This book seeks to engage with a range of theoretical perspectives, in order to define children's literature as part of a broader conception of literary engagement and, at the same time, contribute to an understanding of its difference.

Debates surrounding definitions of 'children's literature' (Hunt 1994) and the problems which arise when studying children's texts within a theoretical framework are continually engaged in the effort to balance the literary and pragmatic aspects of the subject. Whether in order to correct the assumptions of children's books as simple, to enrich the reading experiences of 'real' children (Nodelman 1992), or to challenge the marginalisation of the subject in the academic mainstream (Hunt 1991; McGillis 1996), literary theory has transformed the way in which children's literature is studied. More significantly, feminist theory, psychoanalytic theory and a wide range of reader-orientated theory has awakened critics to cultural constructions of 'the child' (Rose 1994; Lesnik-Oberstein 1994), and the ways in which children's texts function in relation to such constructions.

There can be, however, a reluctance on the part of some critics to perform literary surgery on the beloved texts of childhood, suggesting a need to preserve a sense of magic surrounding children's books that might draw scholars to them in the first place. Many of the tensions involved in teaching children's literature as a literary subject have to do with the necessity of escaping, for a time, from the nostalgic pleasures of revisiting a well-loved story. The development of an understanding of the importance of these books as vehicles for artistic endeavour, or as expressions of aesthetic concerns common to all literature may challenge the remembered experience of reading 'as a child'.

For example, rereading Kenneth Grahame's *The Wind in the Willows* (1908) or, indeed, discovering it for the first time as an adult, can offer a return to a comforting and less complex world. However, reading it as a student of literature, particularly through contemporary theory, will awaken the text as a particular response to the society of the early twentieth century. The possibility of darker and more disturbing truths unveiled by such an exploration of the narrative may disrupt earlier, more comfortable readings, but also places the text within the tradition of *fin de siècle* writing.

Discovering that one's favourite authors were perhaps unhappy; that they may have written into their children's fantasies unsatisfied desires and a bleak world view, undermines the image of children's books as a relief from, rather than a disguised expression of, the tensions of adult life. Such discoveries, however, can be seen to enrich the texts as art objects and allow them to be seen in relation to other artistic responses to individual experience.

The fact that children's books are, indeed, written and often read by adults complicates their situation within literary studies. The status of the last volume of Philip Pullman's 'His Dark Materials' trilogy, *The Amber Spyglass* (2000), points to the complexity of the position of children's literature in contemporary society. The debates surrounding the book's contention for the Booker prize demonstrate the widely contrasted perceptions of children as readers, reflecting views about the separateness and assumed inferiority as 'literature' of children's books voiced through the history of publishing for children. Pullman himself challenges this separation, claiming a continuity of readership that is reflected in the sales of his trilogy throughout the world.

Many writers admit that they do not write expressly for children, but find that what they want to say results in a children's book. George MacDonald famously declared that 'I do not write for children, but for the childlike, whether of five, or fifty, or seventy-five' (1905). In so doing, he suggested a definition of children's literature in terms of a way of reading. To be childlike, according to MacDonald, is to be open and receptive, and it is this quality which his fiction demands of his readers. C.S. Lewis made similar claims that, at fifty, he could read fairy tales without a fear of childishness (Lewis 1973), implying that books written for children must be considered in relation not just to a young readership, but with regard to all readers. The situation is made more complex by the vagaries of the publishing industry. Neither the works of Maurice Sendak, nor Richard Adams's *Watership Down* (1973), for example, were originally written expressly for children, although children's publishing houses published them. However, they have become children's classics, due to the fact that their subject matter – children, animals – and their themes, about the search for independence, or the finding of 'home', were attractive to publishers of children's books and not to publishers of adult books. The tendency to define audience in such a restrictive way contributes to the marginalisation of the texts themselves, and the area of literary production as a whole.

Aside from the fact that some authors known for their adult fiction find themselves writing texts for children, such as Toni Morrison, Fay Weldon and Ian McEwan, the world of 'real' literature and the world of children's literature have been kept largely separate. Books for children have, until very recently, been relegated to the realms of the popular and, therefore, they are often outside the remit of the literary critic. While the depth of historical and bibliographic research and the diversity of approaches mentioned earlier might be similar in the two spheres, they are kept largely distinct. Whereas it is not necessary to announce that your book is about Virginia Woolf *and* Literary Theory, for instance, it appears to be necessary to announce the fact when combining the arcane discourses of theory with children's texts.

Titles such as *Criticism, Theory and Children's Literature* (Hunt 1991), *Children's Literature and Contemporary Theory* (Stone 1991) or *Children's Literature and Critical Theory* (May 1995) attest to a need for the subject to justify a place for itself within the literary mainstream. While the development of a critical discourse for the subject has contributed significantly to the ways in which children's texts can be understood, the adoption of literary theory in discussions of children's literature does not go far enough. In order to understand how texts written for children contribute to literature as a part of cultural production, it is necessary to consider the ways in which the power relationship between author and reader is embedded in such texts. By studying children's literature in relation to literary movements, the authors intend to contribute to an understanding of the way children's books show how such power relationships shift over time.

The choice of texts

This book's focus is solely Anglo-centric, yet the importance of children's literature to any national tradition should be acknowledged. There are certainly other histories to be written, but it is possible to view British and American children's literature, particularly, as a relatively homogeneous body of work, reflecting many shared concerns, and enlivened by international influences. However, while German, French and Scandinavian fairy tales in translation contributed to early debates about the nature of a literature for children, it is only rarely that works in translation are made available to young readers in English-speaking countries. Similarly, contemporary children's literature has been influenced by a wealth of African and Indian folk literature, yet work by contemporary writers is rarely published in English-speaking countries.

There is a degree of diversity within those linguistic limits, and many scholars focus on the particularities of national identity and diversity, yet there is a sense of a shared tradition of children's literature written in English. The interconnectedness of British and American children's literature is acknowledged in the texts chosen for discussion. While much is shared in the publishing histories of these two traditions, and all of the texts discussed have been available in both Britain and America, there are marked differences in cultural definitions of 'the child', and the discourses which surround children's literature between Britain and North America.

In fact, the history of American Literature has, from its beginnings, been taunted with accusations of its childishness, and was thus belittled within the mainstream of literary study. Most famously, D.H. Lawrence and Henry James both accused American writers of naïvety, in comparison to the complexities of the European tradition. The emphasis on finding a new and original voice for a new nation contributed to what might be described as a naïve voice, and the work of many home-grown writers blurs the boundaries between child and adult audience. Yet the search for originality also contributes to the place of American children's texts at the forefront of innovation and challenge, often in response to the literary traditions of Europe, which predominated in the American publishing industry until late in the nineteenth century. In addition, the cultural value of childhood in America offers useful comparisons with that of Britain, and thus provides evidence of the extent to which such values are embedded in the books children are given to read. The interweaving of these two histories must, however, be acknowledged, and while American texts are included in the following discussion, the emphasis is on a shared sense of literary development and change.

The structure of the book

The book is structured in five sections. Each section contains a general chapter, tracing a stage in the history of literature. As discussed above, these chapters will not include exhaustive lists of texts but will explore notions of authorship, definitions of childhood, and the ways in which children's texts respond to world events and changing perception about the relationship between the individual and the social world. Because we want to emphasise the extent to which children's books are *about* writing for children, stylistic innovation and the importance of narrative will be of major concern.

Following each general chapter are two or three shorter chapters, each providing a close reading of one children's book and the ways in which it reflects the concerns of the literary movement or period discussed in general. For example, the chapter on Romanticism is followed by a discussion of Ruskin's *The King of the Golden River* and a chapter on *Little Women* by Louisa May Alcott. Although neither of these books was published until the nineteenth century, they each engage with notions of childhood and authorship derived from the Romantic period.

The intention of these readings is to show a variety of examples of the significance of particular children's books to particular literary movements. By providing detailed examinations of individual texts, we wish to suggest ways of reading other children's books within a critical and historical context. These texts have been chosen for a variety of reasons, but mainly because they are of particular interest to the authors of this book. Many of these books will be familiar, but some will be less so. Other works could have been chosen with equal relevance, but those selected provide evidence of the complexity of children's books and each contributes to an understanding of authors writing *about* writing for children. From John Ruskin to Philip Pullman, each author demonstrates, through narrative strategy and voice, a conception of 'the child' as both an idea and an audience. In this way, each discussion provides a way of studying children's books, in order to understand the relationship between author and reader, and how that relationship responds to the aesthetic of particular literary movements.

The books have also been chosen to provide a range of texts from both Britain and the United States of America, in order to show the extent to which each nation responded to change and to examine the sharing of inherited values. In addition, we have attempted to embrace a range of critical discourses, which enrich the ways in which it is possible to consider children's texts. Some readings may focus on the importance of a gendered reading to a particular literary movement, while others concentrate on the way in which a growing interest in psychoanalytic thought influences a text.

Finally, we provide a selective bibliography, which includes a range of approaches with which to enrich this history. Again, this is not intended to be exhaustive, but encompasses a range of theoretical, historical and cultural reading, which may suggest further investigations and, perhaps, challenges to the readings offered here.

It is hoped that the combination of the broad canvas, the individual close readings and the bibliographies will lead readers of this book to explore children's books more closely and, what is more, understand their relevance for an understanding of the role of literature in reflecting and shaping individual experience.

Section 1

Romanticism

Chapter 1

Imagining the child

The fascination with childhood and a desire to recapture an innocent apprehension of the world are key features in any definition of Romanticism. It is often claimed that the image of the romantic child has been a key point of reference for the birth of children's literature since the beginning of the nineteenth century. Myers (1992) states, for instance, that 'the Romantic child is our foundational fiction' (cited in Plotz 2001: 45).

It is the idealised relationship between adult author and child reader, formed out of the Romantic aesthetic, which serves as a model for subsequent writing for children in English. All children's literature, since its inception, engages in some way with this relationship, whether as a celebration of it, or in terms of its impossibility. The authors discussed in more detail in this study are particularly interesting because they consciously address the inequality at the heart of the adult author/child reader relationship.

The emphasis placed on the unsullied freshness of childhood during a period of great change, must be seen as a key factor in the creation of a literature that directly addressed children as audience, through a direct appeal to the imagination. Whether inspired by Wordsworthian notions of the babe, 'trailing clouds of glory', or Ralph Waldo Emerson's view of children as models of a transcendental response to American society, the idea of the child is central to any culture's conception of itself.

The idea of the child constructed during this period cannot be separated from the continual adult questioning and contemplation of the relationship between the individual and society and with God. At the same time, children, both collectively and as individuals, were at the centre of more pragmatic debates about education and the inculcation of moral values. The views of many thinkers of the day, expressed through educational treatises, poetry and fiction for both adults and children, express the conflicts surrounding what adults should 'say' to children that are still familiar today.

Literature produced for children has always been influenced by debates originating in the eighteenth century. The desire to protect innocence or to control wayward thoughts; to balance education and enjoyment; and to preserve childlike qualities into adult life is familiar in the most contemporary of contexts. Childhood, as a time of play and irresponsibility, can be seen as a challenge to, or escape from, a world that privileges reason, progress and strict codes of morality and behaviour. More importantly, the idea of childhood around which these debates are contested originates in Romanticist thought.

Books about children's literature frequently use the term 'Romantic' to describe either the child-as-character, the children-as-readers or the texture and mood of many fantasy works of the nineteenth century. Even though contemporary fiction for children is referred to in the same way, the label is at once too precise to be used in this way, or not precise enough. Romanticism needs to be recognised as an aesthetic and philosophical tendency; an expression of dissatisfaction with what had come before, during the Age of Reason. Romantic ideas were also a response to the revolutionary upheavals occurring on both sides of the Atlantic during the late eighteenth century.

While this tendency appeared to embrace reform and to celebrate individual freedom and self-expression, the individual voices responding to the mood of the time were not always in agreement. At times, particularly in regard to reactions to the debacle that was the French Revolution, views expressed by key Romantic figures, such as Wordsworth, seem reactionary or perverse. It is therefore important to acknowledge that issues surrounding children, education and literature were part of a continual dialogue between contesting agendas, rather than a single set of ideas. The influence of Romantic thought is not expressed purely, but is subject to the heterogeneous nature of both the development of education and the nature of literature itself.

It is impossible to consider Romanticism without addressing the centrality of childhood and the development of a literature specifically for a child audience, but equally impossible to discuss children's literature without investigating the complexity of these debates. From Blake's *Songs of Innocence*, through the poetic contemplations of Wordsworth and Coleridge, the idea of childhood innocence and promise is indivisible from Romantic responses to rationalist thought, revolutionary politics, class and gender shifts, the growth of industrial economy and the transformation of the natural landscape. The growth in democratic politics and a growing consciousness about equal rights on both sides of the Atlantic suggests an inherent connection between imaginative works for children and the trends in female emancipation; a connection that is reflected throughout the history of the form.

The many attempts at children's writing by writers and thinkers of the time, such as the early feminist, Mary Wollstonecraft, among others, also indicated the sense that it was important to engage with these 'innocent' beings through fiction. John Ruskin, whose own work on the history of art and political economy arose out of the roots of this aesthetic, provided a later example of such an attempt. His only work for children, *The King of the Golden River*, influenced by the translations of German folk tales available in English for the first time in the nineteenth century, is discussed in more detail following this chapter.

The history of the production of children's texts and the tensions that continue to arise between what is termed the popular and the literary, can also be said to originate during an age when the growth of the middle class created a lucrative market in publishing for children. Debates surrounding what children *should* read, as opposed to what children *wanted*, are lent a particular poignancy when concerned with commerce, yet the pragmatics of publishing continue to conflict with aesthetic concerns.

The economic realities of the book trade also had an impact on the spread of specifically English children's books throughout the world, and contribute to the shared tradition of American and British children's fiction. The desire of American publishers to struggle against their dependence on British literary production influenced the growth of an exclusively child-orientated publishing industry. Children's books were imported, primarily from England, well into the nineteenth century, rather than developing out of an exclusively 'American' context, although cheaply produced pamphlets were ubiquitous. This situation affected the publication of all indigenous 'literature', as copyright was only levied on home-grown efforts, and so the development of American children's literature relies on similar roots. Notions of childhood embedded in this literature arise out of the same fascination with democracy, change and renewal.

Transcendentalism, the American form of romantic idealism, rose out of the same roots in German Romanticism that influenced the work of Blake, Coleridge and Wordsworth, yet interpreted notions of the sublime in particularly local ways. Thus, in opposing the materialist trend in early nineteenth-century America, Transcendentalist philosophers and poets found a particular relevance in a childlike apprehension of the landscape and the revolutionary project of the American nation.

Originally perceived as a new Eden, the threat posed to the promise and youthful spirit of a new nation by the materialism of industrial progress and control of the wilderness, informed the transcendental response to the societal trend toward conformity, and thus away from the radical origins of America. Jerry Griswold (1992: 69) refers to 'America-as-child' as a powerful trope found in both adult and children's literature, and it is the impulse to reawaken the Adamic spirit that can be found in the idealist construction of childhood.

Whether in England or America, it is necessary to see the children's literature that arose out of ideas first expressed through Romanticism in terms of narrative approach as well as subject matter. A fascination among poets and thinkers of the day for speaking to children through fairy tale and fantasy challenged the prevailing trend for moralistic stories with an evangelical emphasis, and suggested a new way of perceiving the child-as-audience. The Evangelical emphasis on catechism called for a literature that fulfilled a need to address the innate sinfulness of children, and provided a literature based on instruction and improvement. In a similar way, rationalist doctrines claimed, with reference to John Locke's sense of *tabula rasa*, that children were blank slates on which to write.

Although the inculcation of dominant values remains within the discourses which surround children's literature as an educational and moral tool, Romantic adherence to a natural connection between children and higher truths opened the way for a new means of communicating through fiction. Literature that arose out of this tradition offered not only content based on fantasy and dream, but also a form based upon the expectation that children as listeners or readers possessed an unspoken understanding of the sublime and hidden meaning at the heart of the imaginative process.

By championing the fairy tale and celebrating fantasy as the most appropriate form of children's literature, many Romantic writers opposed the instructional and moralistic tales of, amongst others, the Religious Tract Society. Wordsworth, Coleridge and others, proposed subject matter to which children should be exposed, but more importantly, suggested a new way for adults to speak to children. The oral roots of the folk and fairy tale made them a particularly useful model for a narrative voice, which spoke to a shared audience. If childhood is considered to be a state of heightened sensitivity to all things spiritual, rather than something to be grown out of and improved upon, then the fairy tale also attracted those who wished to recuperate the child-sensibility in themselves.

Although it is frequently stated that folk tales and fairy tales were not originally intended for children, but for a primitive, uneducated audience, the participatory nature of oral narrative served as a corrective to the authoritarian paternalism of instructional texts. A narrative contract which offers an open text and invites the reader to share in the making of meaning implies a different relationship between author and reader, which is more democratic in approach, nurturing an imaginative spirit rather than controlling and enforcing particular ideologies.

Of course, it would not be true to suggest that there is a strict opposition between the controlling narrative of the moral tale that talks down to children and an open text that offers the reader a more active position. The heterogeneity of the fiction of the period encouraged a kind of hybridity, so that the more generous narrative voice could be used to good effect in an instructional text and a fantasy setting could be used for didactic purposes. Charles Kingsley, in *The Water-Babies* (1863), for instance, voices the invitation for his child readers to make their own sense of the story, yet his moral intent is clear to his adult readers. The notion of fantasy appealing directly to the child's susceptibility to the sublime has come to be read as a central tenet in Romantic thought, and has contributed to the primacy of the literary fairy tale, particularly in the latter half of the nineteenth century.

> In assigning the fairy tale an absolute origin, and thus lending it a transcendent status beyond criticism, the early Romantics set the tone for many of the literary studies of fairy tales to follow. The Romantic belief in the fairy tale's unproblematic traditional status and oral, folk origins continues to inform much recent work on the fairy tale and its relation to the history of children's literature.
>
> (Richardson 1994: 124)

However, as Richardson so persuasively argues, the support of fantasy and fairy tales for children, although founded on notions of freedom and the natural inclination of children to a moral understanding, is continually inflected with the desire to shape and control.

The desire to idealise childhood as a time of 'one-ness' with the spiritual contributed to a literature, proposed by Wordworth and his peers, which 'sought to reconstruct the child's subjectivity as an ordered, legible, normative and moralized text in its own right' (Richardson 1994: 141). While Wordsworth was extremely vocal in his support of fairy tales, he was careful to recommend religious tracts for the children of the poor. The increase in literacy amongst the poor was seen most often as a threat by those who had experienced the uprising of the labouring classes in France, as well as smaller rebellions on English soil, such as the Swing Riots of the 1820s (Butts, 1997). Whilst the child of nature, the familiar child of whom Wordsworth writes in *The Prelude*, reflects the Romantic image of the angel, the unblessed child must be controlled and kept from undermining the child whose natural place is 'as father to the man' ('My Heart Leaps Up').

Thus, it is always the adult need to ascribe to themselves a childhood that is somehow connected with the sublime, which influences the literature that arises out of a Romantic ideology. Support of fairy tales can be read, particularly in the autobiographical account of Wordsworth's childhood, *The Prelude*, through a gloss of memory, in an attempt to regain a sense of wholeness and spiritual unity, interrupted by the demands of adult (and prosaic) life.

While children exposed to the didactic books of the day, like the boy in *The Prelude*

Can string you names of districts, cities, towns
The whole world over, tight as beads of dew
Upon a gossamer thread; he sifts, he weighs;
All things are put to question; he must live
Knowing that he grows wiser every day
Or else not live at all . . .
                                (1850, Book V 320–325)

Wordsworth calls out for fairy tales, which act 'on infant minds as surely as the sun /Deals with a flower' (352). The pairing of stories and Nature implies a direct connection with children, and it is this essential organic paradigm of the child as a plant, introduced by Rousseau, that lies at the heart of Romantic contemplations of the child. At once suggesting spiritual origins and challenging notions of original sin, the use of natural tropes to validate radical projects for education reacted against the emphasis on fact-based education. Though Rousseau did not espouse reading for young children, his influence is clear in the poetic expression of the essentialist image of the child in nature, which we have inherited from the Romantics.

In *Emile* (1762), Rousseau challenged the traditions which viewed children as potential adults, and presented a revolutionary, but simple, view that celebrated the natural tendencies of childhood and demanded that they be celebrated and nurtured, rather then directed toward adult values and knowledge. To Rousseau, children were natural prodigies, imbued with a 'quasi-divine nature which renders it superior to adults' (Richardson 1994: 11). Healthy maturity could not be reached without a childhood in which the child is allowed to grow as it will. Books, by and large, were anathema, aside from Defoe's *Robinson Crusoe*, which taught self-sufficiency and survival in the natural world. Even Aesop's *Fables*, a staple of light-hearted moral teaching, were unacceptable, for Rousseau recognised that children were subversive readers and likely to read against the pedagogic intention. The child's natural resistance to such controls, however, was to be celebrated, for it is only in childhood that one's sense of self is formed. Certainly, the tension between the degree of control and freedom is continually played out in children's literature throughout its history.

Though the response to Rousseau's proposals for child-rearing ranged between angry rejection and celebratory acceptance, the intense debates around control and freedom were particularly relevant during a time of social and political upheaval. 'The construction of childhood in an age of revolution and reform is neither a politically disinterested nor an ideologically neutral matter' (Richardson 1994: 24). The desire to question the place of the individual within a society in flux; the anxiety arising from the disruption of the hegemony; the shift in class structure and the need to negotiate constant shifts from rural economies to industrial capital, all impinged on the ways in which childhood was constructed.

In addition, improvements in child health and the consequent drop in infant mortality rates transformed the way in which adults viewed childhood. The trend toward educating children outside the family and the shift of child labour, from helping on the family

farm to working in mines or factories, also contributed to the
perception of children as different to adults. On the one hand, these
prosaic realities created a firmer connection between parents with
their individual children. On the other, they suggested a conflict
between the perceived purity of children and the growing material
concerns of the world that contributed to a view of the abuse of
innocence.

The poet and visionary, William Blake, offered a radical challenge
to the treatment of children in the eighteenth century. His writings
reflected his belief in the ability of children to see the attempts of
the adult world to control and misuse them, and provided a powerful argument for the politicisation of education. While there is continual debate concerning the intended audience for *Songs of Innocence*,
it must be acknowledged that their *use* as children's poetry speaks to
perceptions of children innately equipped to understand the invitations to interpretation at the heart of poems like 'The Lamb'. For, if
the simple cadences and pleasant rhymes of the songs may seem
accessible to the less sophisticated reader, it is the openness and trusting generosity of Blake's spiritual vision that counteracts the tendency to teach through verse in the *Divine Songs* of Isaac Watts, for
instance. What is more, the juxtaposition of the paired poems of
Innocence and Experience encourage the adult reader to create an
ironic text which speaks out 'against what he perceived as deforma-
tive influences, such as the prudential and providential morality of
the mercantile classes, well summed up for young readers in the
worldly little proverbs of Newbery's *Little Pretty Pocket Book*'
(Summerfield 1984: 228). Thus, through an appeal to children as
readers, Blake is able to construct childhood as a time of visionary
innocence. At the same time, his poetry can challenge adults through
ironic counterpoint to question the importance of retaining that
innocent consciousness. The implications the loss of that knowledge
might have for the adult psyche and the social world lie behind the
tension of speaking to children through literature and can be seen to
influence children's writers throughout its history.

Childhood was thus idealised by those who were concerned with
retrieving a consciousness of the sublime; of recapturing knowledge
and feeling of those truths unknown and unspoken. The transcendental awareness, which could be interpreted as closeness to God,
was as natural and familiar as mother's milk to the infant, as De
Quincey claimed, and was sought by those who espoused a Romantic
ideology. A growing consciousness of the distance between a child-

like apprehension of the universe and adult experience lent a mood of melancholy to much writing *about* childhood at the time. However, the possibility of regaining or recuperating a childlike vision informs the motivation behind much of the poetry and the support for fairy tales and fantasy by Romantic poets generally.

The connection between stories and mother's milk (Mellor, 1993) suggests the power of the feminine voice within children's literature that can be seen to originate in Romantic thought, along with the notion of mother as the primary nurturer and educator. It is important, however, to define 'the feminine' not in terms of the gender of the author, but with reference to the notion of the feminine in terms articulated by feminist critics of the late twentieth century.

The relevance of contemporary feminist criticism to an understanding of children's literature is well documented (see Thacker 2001, for instance). It is most useful, perhaps, in terms of an understanding of the way that authority is produced or challenged within language, and literature, in particular. Seen in these terms, literary language can act as a challenge to dominant discourses, and it can be persuasively argued that children's literature is included in such subversions.

The relationship of these notions to a Romantic aesthetic is familiar in the reliance of Romantic texts on the sublime and unspoken truths to which children are naturally receptive. The privileged position of childhood in relation to these truths 'beyond language' can be seen to originate from the Romantic constructions of childhood from which the literary tradition derives.

The French psychoanalyst and theorist, Julia Kristeva, offers an interpretation of Lacanian psychoanalysis which is particularly relevant for the children's literature theorist (Thacker, 1996). In her model of the poetic discourse, she makes use of Lacan's reinterpretation of Freud to associate poetic language with a challenge to the dominant order. The power of the *imaginary*, a period during which the baby and the mother are physically close, such as during breastfeeding, is replaced, during the educative process, by the *symbolic order*, or the realm of language. In psychoanalytic terms, this process imposes the 'masculine' law of language systems upon a more sensual and creative relationship with sound in the 'feminine' domain of the *imaginary*. For Kristeva, it is the bubbling up of these more fluid and ambiguous uses of language from underneath the rule-based system of language that lead to the creation of poetic language.

The Romantic ideal of the relationship between childhood and stories suggests a search for the 'feminine' voice that endures throughout the history of children's literature, and characterises its subversive potential. The struggle between the educative function of books written for a child audience, and the need to nurture the imagination is continually played out in this history, influenced by the play between 'masculine' and 'feminine' influences in society as a whole.

Whereas the conflict between the feminine and the masculine, the imagination and reason, is often considered as a direct opposition between rationalists and the Romantics, the importance of play was acknowledged specifically by Locke, although he espoused the philosophy of reason and rationalism. William Godwin, too, husband of the proto-feminist, Mary Wollstonecraft, and father of Mary Shelley, sought a reasonable compromise, arguing for the freedom of children both to experience reasoning and to exercise the powers of their imaginations. Though refusing to assign children with the transcendental knowledge claimed by the Romantics, Godwin urged an acknowledgement of the individuality and independence of spirit of children. However, he also viewed the child within a continuous process of development toward reasoning adulthood and, thus, did not call for a return to the childlike. Rather, he looked toward a socially responsible maturity, as opposed to attempts to regain lost innocence. Again, the notion that children's literature is something to 'grow out of' is under continual public debate.

In general, it is the rationalist urge to inculcate adult values in the education system and the moralistic texts of the time, which was seen to militate against the growth of natural innocence and a 'childlike' engagement with the natural world. Writers such as Mrs Barbauld, with her instructional and devotional books for children, for example *Hymns in Prose for Children* (1791), met the evangelical need to impress devotional feelings upon children. Similarly, the severity and moralising tone of *Divine Songs* (1715) by hymnist Isaac Watts, were considered by more radical thinkers of the day to be detrimental to inborn tendencies toward good. It was as if the very act of imposing knowledge or enforcing ideologies destroys primary knowledge of transcendent truths, which are thus hidden from the conscious mind.

In America, Ralph Waldo Emerson, too, claimed that a child's ability to see through 'fresh' and innocent eyes was disrupted by society and, thus, could only be regained through contemplation of nature.

To speak truly, few adult persons can see nature. Most persons do not see the sun. At least they have a very superficial seeing. The sun illuminates only the eye of the man, but shines into the eye and heart of the child.

(Emerson 1998: 6)

The ability of the child to stand apart from society and to resist being 'clapped into jail by his consciousness' (1998: 147) provided a useful trope for Emerson's transcendental call for nonconformity that is recognisable in many enduring American children's books. Poets and writers who found his Transcendental philosophy more welcoming than the Puritan and Calvinist teaching that Emerson challenged, attempted to adopt a childlike apprehension of nature. It is possible, in the works of Emily Dickinson or Henry David Thoreau, for instance, to trace a note of optimism that one could recapture such an innocent vision, become 'a transparent eyeball' and see as a child. While British Romanticism focuses more on the idealised innocence of adult memory, the idealist philosophers in America reflected a perception of America as a new world, which required a freshness of vision to prevent it from becoming like the old world. Parallels with youthful revolt against parental restrictions can be seen in the relationship between the two countries and this contributed to a sense of childishness in the American literary works of the mid-nineteenth century. *Little Women* (1868), by Louisa May Alcott, which is discussed in more detail in a later chapter, is a perfect example of such a text. Now celebrated as an expression of female selfhood, the reputation of *Little Women* suffered from its status as a children's book, although it was also read by adults. Its focus on children growing up, and its optimistic vision of the possibilities of self-reliance and nonconformity, had consigned it to the margins until its recuperation by Elaine Showalter (1991). Although the tenets of Transcendentalism remain below the surface, Alcott's heritage is reflected in the March family's philosophy, and it is Jo's ability to bring her freshness of vision to the school she runs at the end of the book, which reflects an optimism typical of American children's fiction.

The English tradition suggested a distinction between the child as a signifier for a childlike apprehension of the world, and the recollection of innocence, so familiar to readers of Wordsworth, considered by many critics to be the most powerful influence on the way we now think about and write for children. His contemplation of childhood, within his poetry, and its contribution to notions of selfhood, in addition to his vociferous support of fairy tales and fantasy for children, inform the consistent concern with the unknowable in children that contributes to the complexity of children's literature. For while he led the campaign, continually revisited, for a literature that would contribute to the child's innocent vision; he was also always concerned with the ways in which child experience was transmuted by adult influence.

Thus the dangers of rationalist modes of education contributed to dislocations in one's sense of self, just as the encroaching industrial landscape disrupted the ability to regain that sense in natural landscapes. Those who sought to speak to children, either through catechistic methods of education or through religious tracts and moral tales, were in danger of destroying the unspoken and spiritual knowledge that lay beyond the reach of the mature mind.

> Rather than seeking to infiltrate the child's mind, Wordsworth and Coleridge propose that the child be left by itself to confront gaps and limitations in its habitual thinking process; the child's psychic growth will be stimulated by its own dissatisfaction with, or puzzled sense of something missing in, its conscious identity, rather than remorselessly guided through a graded and normalized developmental schema.
>
> (Richardson 1994: 57)

This opposition between imposed knowledge and the possibility of discovery through an open apprehension of the world, lies at the heart of the development of a literature specifically for children. Whether to instruct, or to attempt to reach an inexpressible understanding attributed to 'the Romantic child' through fiction, is a question that is continually played out in the history of children's literature, inflected by changing aesthetic concerns and conceptions of the self.

The chapters that follow provide examples of the influence of Romantic thought on two children's texts, beginning with Ruskin's fairy tale, *The King of the Golden River* (1850 in Wilmer 1997). While, as I have argued, it is possible to examine the influences of Romantic thought in most 'classic' children's literature, the preoccupations with the fairy-tale form and the sublime in nature, as well as the relationship between political economy and morality, are particularly evident in Ruskin's tale. Second, the discussion of

Alcott's *Little Women* (1994) focuses on the Romantic idealism reflected in the development of the character of Jo March. Each text, although written in the nineteenth century, demonstrates the extent to which the project of writing for children is influenced by Romantic thought of the previous century.

Chapter 2

John Ruskin's *The King of the Golden River* and Romanticism

John Ruskin's *King of the Golden River* (Wilmer 1997) employs the form of a fairy tale to interrogate the interrelationship between notions of political economy and morality through the philosophical position of Romanticism. There is also a correlation between Ruskin's personal experiences and his fairy tale.

John Ruskin (1819–1900) was an influential nineteenth-century art critic and social philosopher. *The King of the Golden River* was his only piece for children, and was written as a gift for the thirteen year old Effie Gray, who was later to become his wife. Thus he was consciously writing to a child reader. The tale was written in 1841 on his return from a European tour; however, Ruskin did not publish it because he considered it unimportant. His father decided to publish the tale in 1850, a fortuitous decision on his part. The work proved successful, and was popular throughout the nineteenth century. It is important in literary terms because it is regarded as the one of the first English literary fairy tales. From a contemporary reading, it is clear that the ideas Ruskin was to develop in his later political and philosophical work are contained in cameo in *The King of the Golden River*.

The literary qualities clearly reflect the perspective of Romanticism: for example, the importance of nature; the relationship between the characters and their surroundings; the moral oppositions of the socially constructed landscape and the natural landscape and seeking the sublime experience through nature. The work also reflects a political awareness. Childhood is perceived as a site of innocence, where the child learns by experience. The imagination is of central importance, and is a place where other worlds are made outside the constraints of the real.

Romantic writers had particularly supported fairy tales as being important to childhood reading, at a time when other writers coming from an educational perspective preferred a more directly didactic mode. Ruskin had read Grimms' fairy tales as a boy, furthermore he wrote the introduction to a new edition of Edgar Taylor's *German Popular Stories* (1868), in which he emphasised the importance of the capacity of the traditional tale to be able to animate 'the material world with inextinguishable life' (Wilmer 1997: 47). It therefore seems pertinent that Ruskin should choose to write a fairy tale modelled on the Grimms' tales as his only piece for children. Ruskin noted this influence in his biographical work *Praeterita* (Ruskin 1885), remarking that *The King of the Golden River* was 'a fairly good imitation of Grimm and Dickens mixed with a little Alpine feeling of my own' (Rahn 1985: 1).

As we have seen, there is a clear connection to be made between the events of Ruskin's personal life and the tale. When he was a student at Oxford, Ruskin had suffered what would now be termed a breakdown. His parents took him on a European tour in the hope that he would recover. It was not until they reached the Alps that he began to regain his health, hence his reference to his sense of a 'little Alpine feeling of my own'. Ruskin records the experience in *Praeterita*:

> I woke from a sound tired sleep in a little one-windowed room at Lans-le-bourg, at six of the summer morning, June 2nd, 1841; the red aiguilles on the north relieved against pure blue – the great pyramid of snow down the valley in one sheet of eastern light. I dressed in three minutes, ran down the village street, across the stream, and climbed the grassy slope on the south side of the valley, up to the first pines.
>
> I had found my life again; – all the best of it . . .
>
> (Ruskin 1978: 33)

John Ruskin had rediscovered himself through the stimulation of the Alpine landscape and through his relationship with nature. This was a centrally Romantic response. Mountainous regions triggered such reactions for other Romantic writers; for example, the Lake District and Snowdon for Wordsworth and Mont Blanc for Shelley. Mountains provided the site for the contemplation of the sublime, inducing the ultimate emotional experience which could not be directly expressed through language. Ruskin was to write later in *Modern Painters* 'Mountains are the beginning and the end of all

natural scenery' (Ruskin 1888: vol. iv, pt.v., ch. 20: *i*). It is therefore not unexpected that he should choose a mountain setting which
comprised his other world of the imagination as he created it in
The King of the Golden River:

> In a secluded and mountainous part of Stiria there was, in old
> time, a valley of the most surprising and luxuriant fertility. It
> was surrounded, on all sides, by steep and rocky mountains,
> rising into two peaks, which were always covered with snow,
> and from which a number of torrents descended in constant
> cataracts. One of these fell westward, over the face of a crag so
> high, that, when the sun had set to everything else, and all
> below was darkness, his beams still shone full upon this water-
> fall, so that it looked like a shower of gold.
>
> (Wilmer 1997: 47)

In comparison, the landscapes of the tales of the Grimm Brothers
are far less individual, and not imbued with a life of their own.
Ruskin's description of the landscape is detailed and specific,
creating an 'actual' place of seclusion, out of real time. However,
embodied in this description are the philosophical constructs of his
own period, so that he can work out his own moral perspective
through the tale. The opening sentences draw the reader upward
to contemplate the mountainous heights, the site of the sublime.
The scene is naturally highlighted by the richness of the setting
sun on the tumbling water producing a natural gold. In *Ad Valorem*
(1860), an essay on political economy, Ruskin wrote against the
reductionism of utilitarianism, epitomised in the phrase he elected
to write in capital letters to emphasise its importance: 'THERE IS
NO WEALTH BUT LIFE' (Wilmer 1997: 222). The very landscape of his fairy tale animates his political philosophy, which is
then played out in the action of the story.

Ruskin's tale reflects his critique of the Victorian period which
was an age of systematisation producing scientific organisation and
industrial, political, economic and agricultural systems. Ironically,
Ruskin himself, to quote David Carroll, 'was one of the great
Victorian systematisers in an age of comprehensive, yet at times,
eccentric system making' (Carroll 1995: 58). The natural systems
described in the landscape of *The King of the Golden River* are by no
means eccentric, but formulate the physical representation of the
morality of the tale:

It was, therefore, called by the people of the neighbourhood, the Golden River. It was strange that none of these streams fell into the valley itself. They all descended on the other side of the mountains, and wound away through broad plains and by populous cities. But the clouds were drawn so constantly to the snowy hills, and rested so softly in the circular hollow, that in time of drought and heat, when all the country round was burnt up, there was still rain in the little valley; and its crops were so heavy, and its hay so high, and its apples so red, and its grapes so blue, and its wine so rich, and its honey so sweet, that it was a marvel to everyone who beheld it, and was commonly called the Treasure Valley.

(Wilmer 1997: 49)

Ruskin was fascinated and enlivened by cloud formations. In *Modern Painters*, (1856), he writes.

How is a cloud outlined? . . . The vapour stops suddenly, sharp and steep as a rock, or thrusts itself across the gates of heaven in likeness of a brazen bar; or braids itself in and out, and across and across, like a tissue of tapestry; or falls into ripples like sand; or into waving shreds and tongues, as fire. On what anvils and wheels is the vapour pointed, twisted, hammered, whirled as the potter's clay?

(Ruskin 1991: 98)

The tension stated here, and in *The King of the Golden River*, is both a political and a Romantic positioning. The opposition is between the freedom which exists in nature, and the systems imposed by industrialisation. The Romantic position supports the natural in opposition to the constraints of society and the imposition of industrialisation. The 'populous cities' are built on the 'broad plains' below the sublime heights of the mountains. The valley is a fragment of Eden, a Land of Canaan under the governance of an agricultural system executed by the brothers. The moral oppositions are incorporated into the landscape, highlighted by the oppositions of the vitality of nature and the utilitarian reductionism of the brothers Schwartz and Hans, who reduce the gift of life to money.

The whole of this valley belonged to three brothers, called Schwartz, Hans and Gluck. Schwartz and Hans . . . lived by

farming the Treasure Valley, and very good farmers they were.
They killed everything that did not pay for its eating
... They worked their servants without any wages, till they
would not work any more, and then they quarrelled with them,
and turned them out of doors without paying them. It would
have been odd, if with such a farm, and such a system of farming
they hadn't got very rich; and very rich they did get.

(Ruskin 1991: 49)

Schwartz and Hans impose a utilitarian system of farming on the
natural riches of the valley and so feed their greed for wealth. They
are harsh and uncharitable to their workers, and to their younger
brother Gluck. Hard times hit the surrounding area, but the
Treasure Valley remains productive due to the especially fortunate
climatic conditions. The brothers have an opportunity, therefore,
to demonstrate Christian charity when confronted by their first
moral test. However the reader knows that they will fail in this,
because Schwartz and Hans have been described as:

very ugly men, with over-hanging eyebrows and small dull
eyes, which were always half shut, so that you couldn't see into
them, and always fancied that they saw very far into *you*.

(Ruskin 1991: 48)

Traditionally the eyes are the windows to the soul: in focusing on
their eyes Ruskin is suggesting that their very souls are closed. By
inference their only desire is to exert power over others. The
youngest brother, Gluck, however 'was as completely opposed, in
both appearance and character to his seniors as could be imagined
or desired' (Ruskin 1991: 50).

He is the child of innocence who is ill-treated by his brothers.
Fair of complexion and temperament, Gluck acts with charitable
love toward the embodiment of the spirits of nature, the South
West Wind, Esquire, and the King of the Golden River. On the
night of the unexpected visit of the South West Wind, Gluck is
in control of the sources of hospitality, the household and the food.

'What a pity', thought Gluck, 'my brothers never ask anybody
to dinner. I'm sure when they've got such a nice piece of mutton
as this, and nobody else has got so much as a dry piece of bread,
it would do their hearts good to have somebody to eat it with

them.' Just as he spoke, there came a double knock at the house door, yet heavy and dull, as though the knocker had been tied up – more like a puff than a knock.

(Ruskin 1991: 51)

The muted sound suggests that the knocker has been lifted by the wind itself, rather than a human hand, preparing the reader for the entrance of the figure of the South West Wind, who is a physical manifestation of the forces of nature. Gluck is kind and generous and so offers his meagre slice of mutton to the distressed visitor. Schwartz and Hans have no charity in their souls, and their rejection of the South West Wind unleashes havoc and ruin upon the valley through natural disaster.

The reaction of the Black Brothers is pragmatic and utilitarian. All they have left are some 'curious old-fashioned pieces of gold plate', hence they become goldsmiths. However, they adulterate the gold with copper. Clive Wilmer notes that:

> Gold is something of a crux in Ruskin's thought. It is valued, rightly, because it is beautiful and durable; it is one of the gifts of nature which man can graciously adapt to his uses. But when it becomes, as it does for the Black Brothers, a source of greed – . . . a token of one man's power over another – then it ceases to have a value that avails for life.
>   . . . Adulteration was for Ruskin, one of the products of capitalism that most clearly condemned it. It showed that the desire for profit could lead the producer to betray his calling – that the capitalist was motivated by selfishness, not by any wish to provide for the community.
>
> (Wilmer 1997: 318)

The King of the Golden River himself is used to draw together the moral conclusions of the tale. The last golden mug, the embodiment of the King, is the device through which Ruskin melds together artistic creation and nature. Gluck rescues the mug/ King by symbolically entering a fiery furnace, thereby breaking the enchantment laid by a more powerful king. Thanks to the boy's heroic and unselfish actions, humanity has triumphed over greed. On being freed the King sets the ultimate trial to all three brothers before disappearing up the chimney in a scene which echoes the Ascension.

Whoever shall climb to the top of that mountain from which you see the Golden River issue, and shall cast into its stream at its source three drops of holy water . . . the river shall turn into gold.

(Wilmer 1997: 62)

The challenge takes the one who succeeds to the mountain top, the place which represents the pinnacle of the sublime experience. The elder brothers, not surprisingly, fail and are turned to stone, ever more to be tormented by the harshness of the elements. Gluck succeeds because he is charitable and has a sense of humanity, although his achievement is not free from suffering. He gives the holy water to an old man, an abandoned, distressed child and a dog, with the final words which reject the desire for riches: '"Confound the King and his gold too," said Gluck; and he opened the flask and poured all the water into the dog's mouth' (Wilmer 1997: 69).

Predictably, the dog transforms into the King and Gluck then learns that his brothers had poured water from the church font into the stream. The response of the King summarises Ruskin's critique of the nineteenth-century Church in England, which, to Ruskin, failed to demonstrate Christian charity: '. . . the water which has been refused to the cry of the weary and dying, is unholy, though it has been blessed by every saint in heaven. . .' (Wilmer 1997: 69).

The purity of the water has been adulterated, hence the King gives Gluck 'three drops of clear dew' from the white leaves of a lily, which he casts into the stream, and a new valley is formed. Gluck's self-sacrifice and charity thereby create a new Eden, fed into rich fertility by the Golden River. The cycles of adulteration and greed have been broken, and a new world is made.

Ruskin's *The King of the Golden River* is a complex fairy tale drawing upon Romanticism and the morality of political economy. Deep in this story for children is the moral and philosophical basis which underpinned Ruskin's thinking – a philosophy of political economy which many see as the seeds of the British Welfare State – something that was not to be realised for almost another century.

Chapter 3

Closing the garret door

A feminist reading of Little Women

Louisa May Alcott was born 29 November 1832 in Germantown, Pennsylvania, an area of America which was a stronghold of Transcendentalist philosophy. In the writing of *Little Women* in 1868, Louisa May Alcott drew upon her childhood experiences and her upbringing, which was dominated by the Transcendental philosophy and idealism of her father, Bronson Alcott. When Louisa May was eleven Bronson Alcott founded a Transcendental community called 'Fruitlands'. Unfortunately the project collapsed after a year of severe practical difficulties for the family, because the gap between the idealised vision of her father and the practical realities of everyday living was too great. Louisa May Alcott transposed the ideals of Transcendentalism into *Little Women*, but combined them with a realistic practicality. In the fictional world of *Little Women* the focus is on the women of the March family, who live out their Transcendental ideals through their everyday lives and achieve a sense of success and happiness, despite the temporary absence of their father, who has left them to join the forces in the Civil War as a chaplain.

The Transcendental values reflected in *Little Women* are derived from Puritanism and a belief in the 'perfectibility of man' (Bradbury and Temperley 1998: 71). The March family strive to create a New Eden in their lives through hard work and the rejection of materialism. Whilst there is a strong sense of individualism, the wishes of the individual are not allowed to become selfish and override the general good of the family. This awareness provides a set of tensions in the text, as the characters endeavour to balance certain responsibilities with their own desires and the needs of the family unit.

The overall circumstances of the family are determined by the absence of Mr March. Although he could have been exempt because of his age, he has decided to obey his moral conscience and join the Northern forces in the war, leaving his wife and four daughters, Meg, Jo, Beth and Amy, to manage without him. Whilst his decision is morally admirable, the practical result is that his wife and four young daughters, aged twelve to sixteen, have to take responsibility for their own economic and practical affairs. The family are not wealthy: their father had previously forfeited their property in a failed effort to help a friend and his army pay is insufficient to meet household expenses, therefore Mrs March, Meg and Jo have to work to provide for the family.

In *Little Women* Alcott created a realist text within which a female community could actively confront the economic and social realities of life. They have to deal directly with matters which would otherwise have been mediated through Mr March as the head of the household. In his absence Mrs March assumes the position of adult authority and becomes their main provider. She also gives her daughters a great deal of love and is their moral guide and influence on their Christian pathway through life. The girls refer to both parents' projected wishes and desired actions *in absentia* to give them a moral framework; they also have the text of Bunyan's *Pilgrim's Progress*, their father's favourite book, as a further support. Alcott makes considerable reference to *Pilgrim's Progress* both through the characters, and structurally in the text itself, with chapter headings which relate to Bunyan's allegory. She particularly emphasises the importance of Bunyan's character Christian's allegorical struggle through this world to find heavenly perfection. The preface to *Little Women* includes a phrase which Alcott has adapted from *Pilgrim's Progress*; Alcott entreats her 'little Book' to 'show to all' 'What thou dost keep close shut up in thy breast' (Alcott 1994: Preface); that her readers might also become better Pilgrims through this life.

The first chapter of *Little Women*, entitled 'Playing Pilgrims', sets the reader on this allegorical pathway, whilst chapters such as 'Beth Finds the Palace Beautiful' reflect the influence of Bunyan's text. The girls refer to themselves as pilgrims, and speak of having played out the story as a repeatedly pleasurable activity. The combination of parental influence, if at a distance, and a morally didactic Puritan text, provides the safe parameters within which Alcott can give the March girls space to explore and develop their own characters and attitudes, as will be discussed later with direct reference to Jo. *Pilgrim's Progress* represents the allegorical ideal, whilst the reader is privy to the realities of life in the March household as parents and daughters strive to reach unattainable perfection.

Louisa May Alcott portrays Mr and Mrs March as characters with high ideals, but with the normal human frailties. (Mr March, as discussed above, has not always been successful, and his decision to join the army has thrown the family into difficulties.) Mrs March is not without her human weaknesses, as she explains to Jo when she has a serious argument with her younger sister Amy because Jo has refused to take her to the theatre – in retaliation Amy has destroyed Jo's manuscript. Mrs March explains to Jo that she too has fought her battles with anger and impatience when Jo asks: 'Mother are you angry when you fold your lips together and go out of the room sometimes . . .?' (Alcott 1994: 78).

Mrs March answers her impatient and hot-headed daughter honestly:

'Yes, I've learned to check the hasty words that rise to my lips and when I feel they mean to break out against my will, I just go away a minute, and give myself a little shake, for being so weak and wicked . . .'

(Alcott 1994: 78)

Mrs March further explains that she drew her sense of control from her husband: 'He helped and comforted me, and showed me I must practise all the virtues I would have my little girls possess, for I was their example' (Alcott 1994: 79). Mrs March projects an image of motherly duty and patience beneath which lies repressed anger; as a mother figure she upholds patriarchal values; as an individual she struggles with the constraints. The confidences she exchanges with Jo demonstrate her understanding and closeness to the trials Jo experiences. It is as though Jo is a young model of what her mother used to be before relinquishing her freedom in accepting the duties of marriage and motherhood.

The characterisation of Jo enables Alcott to engage in a debate on the social construction of womanhood. Jo resists conforming with the contemporary requirements of feminine behaviour as determined by patriarchal norms, a stance which brings reproach from her elder sister, Meg:

'You are old enough to leave off boyish tricks and behave better, Josephine. It didn't matter so much when you were a little girl;

but now you are so tall, and turn up your hair, you should
remember that you are a young lady.'

(Alcott 1994: 7)

As Shirley Foster and Judy Simons observe, Louisa May Alcott's
Little Women 'suggests that becoming a "little woman" is a learned
and often fraught process, not an instinctual or natural condition
of female development' (Foster and Simons 1995: 87).

Jo is positioned between genders; she is an androgynous figure.
Physically Jo is tall and thin. She is ungainly, with large hands and
feet, unlike her sisters who are depicted as having more conven-
tionally delicate and rounded feminine features. Her mannerisms
and behaviour are male rather than female. She whistles, examines
'the heels of her boots in a gentlemanly manner' (Alcott 1994: 6),
and prefers using boyish slang. She is energetic, active and quick-
tempered, longs to fight in the war like her father and plays brother
to her sisters. In short, she is an androgynous echo of her absent
father: Jo is the 'male' in Alcott's reconstructed family. The maleness of Jo is emphasised by the feminisation of her closest friend,
Theodore Laurence, whose schoolfellows shorten his name to the
effeminate 'Dora' and who also calls himself thus, whilst Josephine
chooses to name herself with the male abbreviation of 'Jo'. Laurie
has refined mannerisms, dances well, and though tall, has little
hands and feet. Laurie is trapped in his male household, and Jo in
her enforced feminine role. Their friendship gives them both a place
to escape to and discover themselves.

Jo's principal mode of escape and of self-expression is through
her writing. She is the author of Gothic dramas and stories which
are a highly valued source of pleasure for the family. Jo's passion
for writing could have been presented by Alcott as an individual-
istic self-indulgence; however, it enhances the family's social life,
and also their economic well-being when Jo manages to sell some
of her work. Writing is centrally important to Jo. Amy's destruction of Jo's notebook provokes the severest outburst of anger in the
text. Jo furiously shakes Amy until her teeth chatter, boxes her on
the ear and is 'quite beside herself'. Losing the beloved writing of
a number of years releases an anger in Jo which destroys the
harmony of the household and consequentially results in Amy's near
drowning in a skating accident. Under other circumstances Jo would
have been caring and watchful for her younger sister. Jo's passionate
response to her loss, both in her reaction and the events of the

narrative, unequivocally stress Alcott's adherence to the importance of the expression of individuality and the liberation of the repressed feminine imagination through writing. The Gothic nature of Jo's writing stands in feminist opposition to Bunyan's *Pilgrim's Progress*, the principal moral text adhered to by the March family under the guiding influence of their father. *Pilgrim's Progress* therefore acts as a patriarchal text as opposed to Jo's feminine Gothic romances, for the writing of Gothic romance is traditionally the textual means of escape for women from patriarchal repression.

Besides writing *Little Women*, her realist novel for girls, Louisa May Alcott herself wrote Gothic romance and sensation fiction. Recent critical attention has reappraised these texts, and demonstrates how Alcott was examining the construction of femininity in her fiction for women, as well as for girls (see for example Stern 1996, 1998). Like her fictional creation, Jo, Alcott's Gothic romances helped to support an impoverished family. More importantly they also gave Alcott an outlet for her passionate nature and sense of frustration. Likewise, Alcott enables Jo to realise her repressed self through her exotic fantasies. She is able to enter her own sense of 'otherness' as she writes, and also when she acts out the dramas she has written. For example, Jo enthusiastically demonstrates the various parts at the rehearsal for the melodrama she has written for her sisters for Christmas night. Jo variously becomes villain, hero, witch and beleaguered heroine, each with a convincing and thrilling passion. Furthermore her sisters are tutored by her, and engage to such an extent that their own identities are displaced. As one reads the passages depicting the rehearsal and the performance, it is difficult to distinguish which sister is playing which part. It is as though they become invisible as 'real' people, and are absorbed into the energy of the fantasy. Jo's fantasy world of intrigue, romantic love, deceit and high melodrama becomes their real world for the duration of the play.

The placing of the Christmas melodrama in the 'real' time of Alcott's narrative presents the reader with an intriguing conflict. Christmas is the great day of celebration for Christians, the day of Christ's birth, yet in this Christian household, Alcott's little women are acting out, therefore 'giving birth' to a wholly different drama. They are bringing Jo's inner world of imagination into reality, thereby recreating the Gothic and pagan passions of their sister. Meg, for example, wears a cloak decorated with cabbalistic signs. The potential subversiveness of Alcott's text at this point becomes more apparent when siting the narrative of *Little Women* in a New England community which would have been historically aware of the Salem witch hunts of 1692. However, Alcott elects to mute the potentially explosive subversive power of her text – which was consciously written for girls, not adults – by reducing the scene of Jo's Christmas play to farce. Alcott's feminist doctrine is presented in *Little Women*, yet contained within an acceptable mode for her young audience. The collapse of the drama into laughter returns the experience to play, the inner space of experimentation contained within the constraints and duties of real life. The girls can act out other roles within a world of safety.

In *Little Women* Alcott guides her exemplary family through actual and moral trials which reflect her experiences and probably those of her readers. Jo matures into a woman who is prepared to take up the burdens of adult responsibility and marriage with the sober Professor Bhaer. They set up 'Plumfield', a school for boys, which reverberates with echoes of the real 'Fruitlands' community of Alcott's childhood. As a married woman and teacher of boys, Jo's life is contained within the patriarchal mores of the present with the potential to influence the future generation with her own philosophical and moral stance. She decides to renounce the 'self-indulgence' of writing, although she continues to tell stories to her boys. Symbolically Alcott's central character, Jo, now has a direct narrative influence on a male community, although she no longer retreats to her garret to write fiction which would bring excitement and sensation into her life and the lives of her women readers. Until contemporary times, the woman writer's place has been margin-alised and consigned as 'the attic', the room of her own where a woman could express and liberate herself undisturbed. In *Little Women* Louisa May Alcott playfully enabled her girl readers to look within her inner room, her centre of repressed imagination, and then she decided to close the door on her garret, at least for her younger readers.

Section II

Nineteenth-century literature

Chapter 4

Victorianism, Empire and the paternal voice

The assumption of the innocence of children predominates as an underlying source of emotional power in much of the children's literature which is typically denoted as 'classic'. Some texts, which appear to endure and are reread or alluded to in subsequent books and films for each generation, frequently use children as characters to signify both the loss of innocence, and the possibilities of retrieving a 'childlike' vision.

The redemptive qualities of the angelic infant are an inheritance of Romantic ideologies and continue to inform the children's literature, seeming to some critics to be placed 'beyond the shocks of history' (Plotz 2001: 39). It is this image of the child, constructed by the writers of Victorian middle-class fiction, which also typifies the imagined implied readers of the children's fiction of 'the Golden Age'. This period, beginning in the second half of the nineteenth century, is considered to signify the development of the distinctiveness of children's literature as a form (Hunt 1994), and produced a number of enduring works, such as those by Lewis Carroll and Charles Kingsley, which define a narrative approach which seems to speak directly to children. As Romantic notions of children as closer to the spiritual took hold of the Victorian imagination, so the texts written expressly for children produced multilayered fantasies, which revealed more about the way societies *imagined* childhood, perhaps, than about the reading experiences of *actual* children.

The second half of the nineteenth century is often claimed to be the period which offered a definition of children's literature as entertaining and subversive and produced texts which now attract adult audiences but puzzle many actual child readers. Hunt (1994: introduction) goes even farther, to claim that adults find 'solace' in these texts. Adult perceptions of the children's books of the period reveal the tenacity of a Romantic inheritance, as we attribute our own pleasure and comfort to an imagined child reader (Rose 1994).

Child figures in adult fiction of the period are too numerous to mention, yet they all serve the purpose of challenging the corrupted adult world. Peter Coveney in *The Image of Childhood* (1967) traces the child as a 'symbol of Nature set against the forces abroad in society actively de-naturing humanity' (Coveney 1967: 31). Little Nell, in *The Old Curiosity Shop* (1841), is but one example of the Victorian 'innocent' provided by Charles Dickens, who held his readers in thrall with various child deaths. Little Nell's purity is juxtaposed with the wickedness and greed of the characters encountered by her grandfather and herself in the city, and it is her sacrificial journey to the countryside which brings about her grandfather's redemption. The association of the child figure with nature may be derived from Romantic tenets, but use of the child figure as a redeemer of adults represents a shift in focus. Similarly, Little Eva, in *Uncle Tom's Cabin* (1852), provides Harriet Beecher Stowe with a suitably sentimental weapon against the hard-heartedness of the slaveholders. Her purity and beauty typifies the mid-Victorian image of the angelic child, and it is her deathbed scene, which wrings the tears out of readers, that provides a cathartic reaction to the evils of the world.

> [T]he Victorians sought in literature, especially in narrative, both a diagnostic tool and a cure for social, cultural, and psychical malaises; sought a means of dramatizing a wide variety of dearths, contradictions, and inadequacies characteristic of the 'age of transition', as well as a format for reimagining traditional culture-generating myths.
>
> (Gilead 1987: 302)

Like these heroines, the child-as-reader in the nineteenth century is also defined as a redemptive kind of reader. The perceived ability of children to understand, at some innate level, the messages offered suggests a heightened sensibility and a possible rescue for the troubled adult psyche. While this might not be true of actual child readers, the need to retain an image of the child as some kind of ideal reader can be seen as a motivating force in much of the classic children's literature of the period.

George MacDonald, a visionary writer and key influence on many writers of children's fiction, both among his contemporaries and more recently, defines and attempts to write for an implied reader who embodies the potential of the Romantic child. Both Charles Kingsley and Charles Dodgson (Lewis Carroll) were friends and shared his concern for the preservation of childhood in the face of Victorian realities. In the twentieth century, both C.S. Lewis and Maurice Sendak claim his work as inspirational to their own writing for children, suggesting an inheritance of similar values within a more contemporary frame of reference.

Although MacDonald was concerned principally with fiction for children, his ability to provide generous and open invitations to his readers might be extended to suggest that adults also seek this ideal reading position. In his essay, 'The Fantastic Imagination' (1905), MacDonald prefigures the writing of twentieth-century theorists in their various definitions of the active reader and 'writerly' text. Roland Barthes, the French theorist who came to prominence in the 1970s, draws a distinction between the *lisible* or 'readerly' text, which is characterised by a straightforward 'telling', and the *scriptible* or 'writerly' text, which offers openings and gaps for the reader to join in the making of meaning. Writerly texts are less fixed and, thus, less likely to impose interpretations, enabling readers to question or to bring their own experiences to bear on the text.

In response to the question, 'You write as if a fairy tale were a thing of importance: must it have a meaning?', MacDonald suggests an immediate connection between the reader and the possibility of deeper meaning:

> It cannot help having some meaning; if it have proportion and harmony it has vitality and vitality is truth. The beauty may be plainer in it than the truth, but without the truth the beauty could not be, and the fairy tale would give no delight. Everyone, however, who feels the story, will read its meaning after his own nature and development: one man will read one meaning into it, another will read another.
>
> (MacDonald 1975: 29)

Though one might consider that much of the moralising familiar to readers of Victorian children's literature runs counter to the openness suggested here, it is clear that the history of children's literature can be traced in relation to MacDonald's view of the child-as-reader as potentially responsive to the openness of the text. MacDonald clearly has a message to impart; his text is not completely open to his reader's interpretation and there are 'correct' ways of reading his work. However, MacDonald uses a lack of definition to provide gaps for the reader to fill. In *The Princess and the Goblin*, for instance, the following scene suggests, rather than dictates, the sense of the spiritual.

> The lady and the beautiful room had vanished from her sight, and she seemed utterly alone. But instead of being afraid, she felt more than happy – perfectly blissful. And from somewhere came the voice of the lady, singing a strange sweet song, of which she could distinguish every word; but of the sense she had only a feeling – no understanding. Nor could she remember a single line after it was gone. It vanished, like the poetry in a dream, as fast as it came. In after years, however, she would sometimes fancy that snatches of melody suddenly rising in her brain, must be little phrases and fragments of the air of that song; and the fancy would make her happier, and abler to do her duty.
>
> (MacDonald 1990: 124)

The sense in which the meanings are beyond conscious under-standing is particularly appropriate to the imagined child reader of the late nineteenth century. It is MacDonald's confidence in his ability to 'speak' to children (and for 'the childlike') through fantasy which challenges the more moralising and controlling fictions by, among others, Mrs Molesworth and Mrs Ewing. The desire to offer children open invitations is echoed in children's literature of the period, though the subsequent flow of literary history demonstrates a gradual loss of such confidence.

Much of the enduring children's fiction of this period can be defined in terms of a belief in the innate ability of children to respond to such invitations. This trust is met with narrative strate-gies that invite a dialogic 'sharing' of the storytelling process between author and reader, rather than a controlling, authoritative and colonising relationship. The books discussed in Chapters Five and Six both demonstrate the extent to which narrative intrusion invites the participation of the reader in a playful dialogue with the author. For example, in *The Water-Babies* Kingsley subverts the instructional voice of the author to suggest an element of self-determination.

And what was the song which she sang? Ah, my little man, I am too old to sing that song, and you too young to understand it. But have patience, and keep your eye single and your hands clean, and you will learn some day to sing it yourself, without needing any man to teach you.

(Kingsley 1995: 269)

However, while this belief in the possibilities of the ability of children to respond to such invitations remains as an undercurrent in most memorable children's literature, the confidence of adult authors to provide the art that will, as MacDonald states, to 'wake things up that are in him', becomes increasingly troubled. The tendency to speak, as an adult, with authority about morality and truth, can be seen as central to the project of writing for children since its inception. It is the increasing difficulty of this project that typifies the flow of literary history from Romanticism toward the more cynical view as we approach the Modernist sensibility of the twentieth century.

The appeal of children's literature in the late nineteenth century to an adult readership indicates the desire to find a reading position that awakened a 'childlike' sense of belief increasingly threatened by religious doubt, brought about by social change and the growth in science as the 'new religion'.

Victorian children's books had to speak simultaneously to adult readers who were increasingly anxious, as they grew older, to recover their own childhood selves, lost in time, in the children about and to whom they were reading.

(McGavran 1991: 9)

The promise of a return to an innocent apprehension of a fictional world is perpetuated by the link between the feminine and the child, familiar to the Romantic poets, their focus on the mother as nurturer and the domestic world of childhood as an essentially feminine location.

The dominance of the feminine in the imaginative and creative realm provides a challenge to the growing masculine world of nineteenth-century Britain and North America. At the same time, the struggle for equal rights on both sides of the Atlantic, and the powerful personal presence of Queen Victoria, invited a re-examination of the notion of femininity. Those texts which attempt to idealise the feminised sensibility rely on the child-as-audience responding in some innate way to the maternal spirituality offered by the female figure. MacDonald's own works, again, emphasise the spiritual power of his female characters and in several children's fantasies (*At the Back of the North Wind, The Princess and the Goblin* and *The Princess and Curdie*) he suggests a supernatural quality which offers readers an open and 'writerly' engagement with the moral questions raised by the stories. The character of the North Wind, for instance, is depicted as a woman, her sexuality effectively enhanced by Arthur Hughes' original illustrations, who both mothers and punishes the child, Diamond. The Queen-Grandmother in *The Princess and the Goblin* has magical qualities and provides the princess, Irene, with the power to rescue Curdie, the miner's son. Similarly, it is the female figure(s) in Kingsley's *The Water-Babies* who motivate the spiritual cleansing of Tom. These characters, the Irish Woman, Mrs Doasyouwouldbedoneby and Mrs Bedonebyasyoudid, act as guides to spiritual progress through a recognition of the feminine. The feminine is opposed to a threatening masculinity and suggests a rejection of the masculine world of a large Northern town, and the greed of the male characters. Even *Alice in Wonderland* and *Through the Looking-glass* can be read with this contrast in mind, as Alice confronts a number of ineffectual male characters, but more combative females, such as the Queen of Hearts, in her travels.

> 'Don't be impertinent,' said the King, 'and don't look at me like that!' He got behind Alice as he spoke. 'A cat may look at a king,' said Alice. 'I've read that in some book, but I don't remember where.'
> 'Well, it must be removed,' said the King very decidedly; and he called to the Queen, who was passing at the moment, 'My dear! I wish you would have this cat removed!'
> (Carroll 1992: 114)

In some instances a kind of androgyny is proposed, or, to be more precise, the feminising of a masculine sensibility. MacDonald and Kingsley both propose that it is the female characters that allow the male children they encounter to find redemption. At times, it is as though attaining a feminised sensibility is a return to a prior and superior state of being.

The Kristevan readings of Lacanian psychoanalysis suggested in Chapter One are relevant here – the privileged state, or *imaginary*, prior to the imposition of the *symbolic order*, can be interpreted as the childlike state of being, prior to imposition of a language system. While this state, during which the child is at one with its mother, can be seen as feminine, the law of language is masculine, and endowed with patriarchal power.

MacDonald's sense of the child-as-reader is reminiscent of the Romantic image of the baby at the breast: capable of wonder without the imposition of a system of meaning. The encounters of the Princess with her Grandmother in *The Princess and the Goblin* or Diamond's remembered nonsense song learned at the back of the North Wind suggest an authorial awareness of, or desire for, a child's sensitivity to transcendental meaning beyond language. The flowing nonsense verse, also familiar to readers of Carroll and Lear, challenges the systematic acquisition of language and breaks its laws. Alliterative and rhythmic language such as this can be associated with the pre-symbolic state, especially in the way that it breaks away from the rules of metre and seems determined by sound.

> wake up baby
> sit up perpendicular
> hark to the gushing
> hark to the rushing
> where the sheep are the wooliest
> and the lambs are the unruliest
> and their tales are the whitest
> and their eyes are the brightest
> and baby's the bonniest
> and baby's the funniest
> and baby's the shiniest
> and baby's the tiniest
> and baby's the merriest
> and baby's the worriest
> (MacDonald 1986: 124)

Diamond's ability to make this song, which carries on for several pages, is due to his journey to the Back of the North Wind, which is a kind of Heaven. His childlike spirituality is associated with his ability to find a relationship to language outside of a system. In a sense, this usage becomes subversive, as it is shown to undermine the rationalism and material concerns of the adult world.

Similarly, Kristeva focuses on the power of this feminised awareness: the *imaginary*, to provide a revolutionary force that undermines the systematic structure of the language system defined by the controlling, partriarchal, *symbolic order*. The child, innately aware of these truths beyond language, can thus be seen as a revolutionary force, working against the controlling, colonising power of the adult world of education and conformity.

The worlds of dream, fantasy and nonsense, appear to subvert the rational world in much Victorian children's fiction, most notably, perhaps, in the 'Alice' books of Lewis Carroll discussed in Chapter Six. A shared recognition of the possibilities for redemption through a childlike, feminised and 'natural' apprehension of the world provide a challenge to the forces of money, power, science and urban existence.

Growing awareness in the late nineteenth century about the mistreatment of children is the central irony of the portrayal of children in fiction for both adults and children, and directly influenced writers of children's books (Coveney 1967). Most famously, Kingsley was moved to write *The Water-Babies* after reading of the conditions of working-class children in England. Charlotte Brontë, with *Jane Eyre* (1847) and Charles Dickens, with *Nicholas Nickleby* (1839), *David Copperfield* (1850) and *Hard Times* (1854), found different ways to challenge the abusive school system and the damage that nineteenth-century values did to the sensibilities of young children (Tucker 1999).

The directness of authorial intent, to call attention to the fact of the experience of children, also influenced the sense of dialogue embedded in the direct address of many of the narratives of the period (Hunt 1994). The tendency to address the story to one particular, known, child indicates a contrast to the anonymity of the current market in children's fiction. Familiarity contributes to a sense of shared purpose and emotional power that is frequently lacking in many contemporary children's books.

Carroll's Alice, and MacDonald's and Kingsley's own children become, then, possible ideal readers, and it is the private language and humour which offers the sense of a shared secret. Such a relationship between author and reader provides a different power structure; the reader has a privileged role. Though later in the century this familiarity can become cloying and authors such as Kipling can seem to talk down to the reader, the power of such a direct relationship with the author suggests the possibilities of reading an open text, which leaves gaps for the reader to fill.

Texts such as Kingsley's *The Water-Babies* or Carroll's 'Alice' books, discussed in the Chapters Five and Six, offer narrative relationships between author and reader that are at once subversive and poignant. Many critics and theorists have struggled to identify this particular quality of 'Victorian' children's fiction, and some have attempted to attribute it to the individual psychology of the authors themselves (Knoepflmacher 1998). However, it is more fruitful to view this tendency as part of a general cultural concern amongst the writers and thinkers of the time. The importance of a dialogue through fiction, with an imagined, but actual, child and the need to provide possible worlds through that fiction, must be juxtaposed with the inevitability of the loss of childlike wonder that is perceived to be a consequence of maturity and conformity in adult life.

The realities of life in the nineteenth century: the rapid growth of cities, industrialisation, the growth of the British Empire and the mercantile classes, threaten adult perceptions of the Romantic images of the child-in-nature and imbue children's fiction with a sense of the unattainability of the childlike apprehension of the world.

In America, too, children's literature provides a challenge to adult values and combats the growing fascination with commerce within the nation. Griswold (1992) attributes the challenge to a 'uniquely American' sense of oedipal politics (1992: 69), deriving from the national tendency toward independence. He also emphasises the predominance of realism over fantasy in American children's books of the period (1992: 45). Many of these texts embody, through a focus on familial problems, a critique of adults and their values that darkens as the nineteenth century ends.

For example, Mark Twain's use of gentle irony in his earlier works, such as *The Adventures of Tom Sawyer* (1876), belittle an adult community concerned with propriety and blind to Tom's transgressions, appearing to glorify antisocial behaviour (MacLeod 1994). In the book that followed, *The Adventures of Huckleberry Finn* (1885), however, Twain's jaundiced view of the slave-holding community is uglier, and he never allows the later book to have the satisfaction of the conclusion of a boy's adventure story. By calling attention to Tom's fascination with tales of pirates and heroes, Twain seems to compare the children's fiction beloved of American boys with the far more serious 'adventure' of imprisoning a runaway slave, suggesting that child's play has become a dangerous game.

The narrative voice of many of the texts of classic nineteenth-century literature may be authoritative and playful; familiar yet instructive, but there is always a sense of loss; an awareness that the adult-as-author is on the other side of a void which the child must also inevitably cross.

Part of this sense of loss must be seen in terms of the strength of scientific discourses and, in particular, the influence of Darwinian theories of evolution discussed and debated during the second half of the nineteenth century. Several authors, notably Kingsley and MacDonald, refer repeatedly to these theories in their work, and Tenniel's illustrations to *Alice in Wonderland* make reference to the descent of man. In *The Water-Babies*, for instance, Kingsley refers to a tribe of people who are so wicked in their ways that they evolve backwards, becoming gorillas as their actions become more immoral. Similarly, MacDonald's goblins and their animals evolve into freakish creatures because they live in the darkness.

> Those who had caught sight of any of them said that they had greatly altered in the course of generations; and no wonder, seeing they lived away from the sun, in cold and wet and dark places. They were now, not ordinarily ugly, but either absolutely hideous, or ludicrously grotesque both in face and form.
>
> (MacDonald 1990: 3)

While the impact on religion of Darwin's publications cannot be overestimated, it is the extent to which prior notions of origin and the self were challenged by science that are particularly influential.

Writing for children at this time could thus be seen as an attempt to revisit, recuperate, or rescue the writer from a less hopeful truth. The impact of Darwinian thinking and the proliferation of scientific discourses cast doubt on the spiritual beginnings of mankind. Childhood, thus, became more important as the position of origin and limit and accorded child-consciousness with an even more immediate relation to the adult sense of self. The religious background of many writers for children at the time certainly had an impact on these developments, and Charles Kingsley best expresses the puzzlement surrounding the need for a new way of thinking. The discussion of *The Water-Babies* in Chapter Five provides a closer reading to reveal his attempts to come to terms with the rise of scientific thought.

The sense that a spiritual knowingness in childhood, forgotten or hidden in adult life (and, perhaps, recoverable through a childlike perspective) is replaced by a need to seek the beginnings of the adult self in the child that that adult once was. Many Victorian novelists exposed this search through fiction in various ways (Nelson 1999: 78). George Eliot with *The Mill on the Floss* (1860), Charles Dickens with *Great Expectations* (1861) and both Charlotte Brontë with *Jane Eyre* and Emily Brontë with *Wuthering Heights* in 1847, focus on the childhoods of their characters as a way of 'explaining' their adult actions.

Whilst still reflecting a belief in the innate goodness in the child, Darwinian thought and the painful realisations that it suggested weakened the possibilities of a return to origins. At the same time, however, it encouraged adults to look toward childhood as the key to their own self-awareness.

In North America in the mid-nineteenth century, the figure of the child is also a redemptive emblem, yet the influence of Darwin is less powerfully implicated. This may be due to the tenacity of the inherently optimistic brand of Romanticism that influenced so much of the literary production of the period, as well as the emblematic power of America as a new Eden, embodying a more immediate sense of origin. Griswold (1992) refers to 'America-as-child', and this powerful trope frequently blurs the boundaries between adult and children's fiction in the American canon, imbuing the beginnings of the American literary tradition with a juvenile or naïve quality. Accusations of immaturity by European critics and writers of the nineteenth and early twentieth centuries, such as D.H. Lawrence, call attention to the appeal to the perceived innocence of American readers. The fact that there were both adult and child audiences for works such as Mark Twain's *The Adventures of Tom Sawyer*, Louisa May Alcott's *Little Women*, and Harriet Beecher Stowe's *Uncle Tom's Cabin*, among many others, provides a pragmatic example of the power of the conventions of the child narrative. The appeal of the child as a figure able to become the ideal American is reflected both in character and in the address to the implied reader of the texts.

The work of the philosopher-polemicist, Ralph Waldo Emerson, portrays the child's apprehension of the world as the ideal, in his attempt to reawaken the Adamic spirit in the midst of a rapidly growing materialistic society. The child, or more specifically, the young boy, is a model for a Transcendental approach to the world

which adults have forgotten, 'clapped into jail by . . . consciousness' (Emerson 1998: 77). While adults have only superficial ways
of seeing, children, nonchalant and nonconformist, see 'with the
heart' and understand intuitively the spiritual in nature. Emily
Dickinson, a poet who shared this aspect of Emerson's philosophy,
attempted, particularly in her nature poems, to write as a child in
order to see with a fresh eye. Although this surface naïvety allows
her poetry to be read by readers of many ages, it belies the
complexity of the verse. Along with her hermetic existence, her
approach to experience, revealed through poetry, could also be seen
as a reaction against the materialist tendencies of the adult world.

As in Britain, the innate Romanticism suggested by such expressions becomes continually overlaid by the realities of living in the
nineteenth century. The possibility of achieving the ideal in
the 1840s, when Emerson was speaking and writing, is gradually
replaced by a more pessimistic vision in the latter half of the century
by authors such as Mark Twain. While many critics refer to his
earlier work as portraits of the idyll of childhood existence (MacLeod
1994), it is his use of the child-as-narrator to present an anti-slavery
message that identifies the power of the child as an image of
hope, though not necessarily of redemption. In *The Adventures of
Huckleberry Finn* (1885), Huck's naïve lack of awareness of an adult
consciousness of race allows the reader to understand the innate
goodness of the slave, Jim, contrasted with the socially constructed
systems of slavery. While Twain's book valorises the innocent ability
to see beyond prejudice, he also pessimistically suggests its unattainability. Tom Sawyer, once the model of unabashed boyhood, is
characterised, in the later book, as the potentially 'socialised' adult.
Twain continually calls attention to Tom's dependence on adventure narratives which lead him to prolong Jim's experience
of slavery, suggesting that Tom's education and 'civilisation' act
as the inevitable destruction of innocent consciousness. Imbued
with Twain's own sense of guilt and ironic vision, derived, in part,
from his own childhood experience of life in a slave-holding town
(Fishkin 1998), such a text embodies the growing discomfort at
the heart of writing for children. Adult self-awareness and a growing
sense of alienation makes the need to provide optimistic models of
life and behaviour more difficult to articulate. Even today, the
underlying challenge of *The Adventures of Huckleberry Finn* is misunderstood, its narrative complexity misread and the naïve vision of
the narrator, finally, seems untrustworthy, rather than redemptive.

The tension between images of Romantic innocence and its inevitable loss, and the conscious need to provide a voice of authority, led to a more self-conscious approach to writing expressly for children. The availability of education for all, albeit separated in relation to gender and class, and the construction of a separate market for children's fiction, meant that much writing for a young audience of the late nineteenth century is split along gender lines. The domination of the adventure story for boys and domestic fiction for girls is well documented (Cadogan and Craig 1986; Reynolds, 1990; Hunt 1995, for instance) and, in some senses, remains a convention of the children's publishing industry today.

It is, however, the expression of a multilayered consciousness of the fragility of innocence and the task of literature to protect that innocence that marks many of those texts which retain their currency and their transhistorical power. At the same time, these texts demonstrate the power of narrative to suggest a sense of regret at the heart of the enterprise of writing for children as the century ends.

Lewis Carroll expresses this sense of regret most poignantly, perhaps, in the verses accompanying *Through the Looking-glass*:

Come, hearken then, ere voice of dread,
  With bitter tidings laden,
Shall summon to unwelcome bed
  A melancholy maiden!
We are but older children, dear,
Who fret to find our bedtime near.

Without, the frost, the blinding snow,
  The storm-wind's moody madness –
Within, the firelight's ruddy glow
  And childhood's nest of gladness.
The magic words shall hold thee fast:
Thou shalt not heed the raving blast.
                    (Carroll 1971: 173)

As a Preface to the story, this verse may be taken merely as an invitation to read, but it also reveals a pessimistic view of what lies outside of childish experience, and Carroll's own ability to keep out the dark.

The complexity of narrative structure and sense of a dual audience in so many of the enduring texts of the nineteenth century exemplifies a doubleness on the part of the adult author (Rose 1994). Writing for children is both an attempt to achieve a dialogue with an idealised construct of 'the child' and, more poignantly, about the struggle to make that connection.

While children are often the perceived audience for these texts, adult perceptions of the difficulties at the heart of the project mean that they provide a richer, multilayered reading experience for adults as well as children. Of course, it must be remembered that the childhoods portrayed in fictions, whether based on an ideal or an author's own, are always a fiction; a construction dependent on the Romantic image of the innocent linked to the feminine. The awareness of the adult writer and adult reader of the desire to portray this lost world in fiction deepens the sense of loss. It is the growing self-consciousness of this fictionality that marks the difference in tone in children's literature as we move toward the Modernist period.

Far easier, perhaps, to offer children a more confident and uncomplicated kind of authorship, most familiar in the adventure story, a subgenre that defines the period and exemplifies the masculine quest narrative. Fiction of this period, appealing to both adult and young audiences, promoted the values of Empire, in the works of writers such as R.M. Ballantyne and H. Rider Haggard. Books such as Ballantyne's *The Coral Island* (1858) or Rider Haggard's *King Solomon's Mines* (1885) celebrated a superior definition of 'Britishness' and provided a version of the quest narrative in an unquestioning way. Similarly, school stories, such as Hughes' *Tom Brown's Schooldays* (1856) or Farrar's *Eric; or Little by Little* (1858) offered an unquestioned Victorian value system for the purpose of moulding moral citizens for the future. In America, Horatio Alger, Jr celebrated the materialist aspects of the American Dream in *Ragged Dick* (1868), promoting the notion of the rags-to-riches story and encouraging the American virtues of self-determination.

The colonising force of fiction to inculcate hegemonic ideologies or to reinforce gender roles is powerful through the history of children's literature, yet there are also texts which seek to resist or challenge this controlling process. The element of the fantastic, and the various attempts to speak directly to children in the most enduring texts of the late nineteenth century, offer an appeal to the 'feminine' and an entrenched loyalty to the Romantic image of children of the early part of the century. The two chapters that follow trace the echoes of resistance in the work of Lewis Carroll and Charles Kingsley, both clergymen who found that the challenges of their time were in conflict with their own notions of the relationship between humanity and spirituality. Their own relationships with individual children deepened their senses of conflict and the resulting fantasies, subversive as they were, suggested a response to the disjunction between images of children as innocents and the confusing and corrupting adult world of the period.

Finally, it is important to note the gradual shifts in the pragmatics of children's literature as an exclusive market. The growth of the middle class and the need to produce fiction for a growing youth market motivated and continues to motivate a division between populist fiction and the aesthetic 'art' of literature. As the world of children – the nursery, the schoolroom – grew more separate from the adult world of the parlour and the workplace, so the perception of audiences for fantasy in particular, but children's literature in general, grew more distinct. The influence of state education, not to mention the power of the boarding school, enforced the separation of children from their parents and thus influenced a gradual change from the familiar and loving voice of the author. The response to this separation was a marked division between the anonymous voice of the more populist and sensational fiction exclusively for children and the more arch and playfully self-aware tone in literature for children at the turn of the century.

Chapter 5

Reality and enigma in
The Water-Babies

Brian Alderson states in his preface to Charles Kingsley's *The Water-Babies* (first serialised in *Macmillan's Magazines* 1862–3), that it 'remains one of the most enigmatic of all children's classics' (Kingsley 1995). There are two reasons for this. First, Charles Kingsley, who was a renowned clergyman, social activist and keen naturalist, was endeavouring to place his own thinking in the turbulent religious, social, and scientific debates of the mid-nineteenth century. Second, the interrelationship between content and narrative form in *The Water-Babies* reflects Kingsley's attempts to control the turmoil of the intellectual quest for resolution through a combination of realism and fairy tale.

Kingsley identified the enigmatic nature of his text in his epigraph which asked his reader to 'Come read me my riddle, each good little man:/If you cannot read it, no grown-up folk can' (Kingsley 1995). Kingsley is asking for his text to be read back to him with a male voice, and by so doing he becomes both the author and the desired recipient of his own text. The writing, therefore, becomes a way of listening to his own voice, a way of considering the intellectual puzzles which he formulates in language. If a child is able to read, and therefore make some comprehension of his text, then Kingsley has a hope of working out his puzzles.

Kingsley uses a frame of realism to contain the text. Beginning with realism is rather like beginning a challenging jigsaw puzzle by sorting out the straight edge pieces in order to set the frame. The realist story of Tom, the boy chimney sweep, evolves into a fairy tale, the narrative then becomes increasingly surreal and concludes with a realist closure with Tom as an adult, 'a great man of science' (Kingsley 1995: 182). The overall structure, therefore, is that of the *Bildungsroman*, that is, a novel in which the subject is:

the development of the protagonist's mind and character, as he passes from childhood through varied experiences – and usually though a spiritual crisis – into maturity and the recognition of his identity and role in the adult world.

(Abrams 1993: 132)

The form of the *Bildungsroman* works in two ways: Tom's story demonstrates to the reader, through fantasy, the physical and moral progression of Tom to maturity, whilst enabling Kingsley, in reality, to pursue some sense of solution to his own spiritual and intellectual crises. The source of Kingsley's turmoil was the impact of Darwinism upon his thinking. Darwin's *The Origin of Species* (1859) was at the centre of the debate on evolution and the philosophical conceptualisation of the Creation. Kingsley's first meeting with Charles Darwin in 1854 fired both a personal and intellectual energy. In 1863 he wrote to F.D. Maurice of his reaction to Darwinism:

I am very busy working out points of natural theology by the strange light of Huxley, Darwin and Lyell ... The state of the scientific mind is most curious; Darwin is conquering everywhere, and rushing like a flood by the mere force of truth and fact. The one or two who hold out are forced to try all sorts of subterfuges ... But they find that now they have got rid of an interfering God – a master magician, as I call it – they have to choose between the absolute empire of accident, and a living imminent, ever-working God.

(Kingsley 1883: 337)

Later the same year he wrote to Darwin:

I have been reading with delight and instruction your paper on climbing plants. Your explanation of an old puzzle of mine ... is a master-piece. Ah, that I could begin to study nature anew, now that you have made it to me a live thing, not a dead collection of names. But my work lies elsewhere now. Your work, nevertheless, helps mine at every turn.

(Kingsley 1883: 339)

The influence of Darwinism, as will be discussed in more detail later, is clearly evident in the underwater fairy story in *The Water-*

Babies. Tom both observes evolution in process, for example in the episode of the metamorphosis of the caddis fly, whilst he evolves himself from the amoral child he was in the world above, into a morally sound adult through his experiences underwater.

The initial realist section is set in the real world of dry land where Kingsley engages with the predominantly social debates which interested him; child labour, education, and the lack of provision of clean water for the working classes. As an omniscient intrusive narrator, Kingsley is able to exert control, and thus embed his moral perspective in the text. Tom is employed by Mr Grimes as a chimney sweep's boy, and as such is illiterate, ill-treated and lacking in religious or moral education. His desire is to be like his master: 'And he would have apprentices, one, two, three, if he could. How he would bully them, and knock them about, just as his master did to him' (Kingsley 1995: 6).

Tom's reaction to his circumstances is to replicate his experiences as a model for his future life, in other words, to become a clone of his amoral master. Kingsley is challenging the philosophical position of life as replication, whilst employing the notion that learning is experientially based in relation to the environment. Tom cannot learn from his experiences and change them because he has no moral education. He subsequently has no framework of morality to apply to his situation to bring about change for the better. At this stage he is equated with an unquestioning animal, a donkey which is the beast of burden:

> As for chimney sweeping, and being hungry, and being beaten, he took all that for the way of the world, like the rain and snow and thunder, and stood manfully with his back to it until it was over, as his old donkey did to a hailstorm.
>
> (Kingsley 1995: 5)

Darwinism confronted the Victorians with the question of what divides Man from the animals, since evolutionary theory identified Man as evolving from the Ape. If Man was created in the likeness of God, but God is taken out of the philosophical equation, what then is there to mark the difference between man and beast? It is this very question which underpins Kingsley's text, hence his alignment of Tom with the animal world. Tom's progression, as a child of and in the real world, is toward a more dominant image of bestiality. When he loses himself in the maze of chimneys at

Harthover Place and emerges from the 'pitchy darkness' into the fairy-tale whiteness and purity of Ellie's bedroom Tom is confronted by his self-image in a mirror:

> And looking round, he suddenly saw, standing close to him, a little ugly, black, ragged figure, with bleared eyes and grinning white teeth. He turned on it angrily. What did such a black ape want in that sweet young lady's room?
>
> (Kingsley 1995: 17)

He does not perceive himself as a child, but as an animal. At this stage he has no self-knowledge and cannot recognise his reflection, which is corrupted by the sooty filth of the chimneys. Tom has to enter a submerged fairy-tale world where he can be cleansed and experience a rebirth as a water-baby. Becoming a water-baby is a return to water, the evolutionary source of life. The child Tom is the victim of industrial society, and is consequently hounded out of Harthover House in the style of a fairy-tale chase.

The fairy tale evolves from the realist narrative and thus enables Kingsley to create a world of 'the other' as the site of his engagement with the debate between Darwinism and his religious beliefs. He had to create an alternative landscape, a water-scape of the imagination, in which to confront the conflict which he could not resolve within reality. Tom's physical and moral journey of evolution is guided by a series of female fairy figures; the Irishwoman, his fairy guardian in the earthly world; Mrs Bedonebyasyoudid, her sister Mrs Doasyouwouldbedoneby and Mother Carey.

Mrs Bedonebyasyoudid and Mrs Doasyouwouldbedoneby embody the process of didactic moral education in terms of punishment and reward, in which Tom must engage in order to change. That educative process is also linked with the logic of evolutionary theory in the naming of the two fairies: 'Bedonebyasyoudid' relates to past action, whilst 'Doasyouwouldbedoneby' determines current action in relation to the best desired outcome. Evolution is about adaptation, i.e. learnt relationships to produce the best current outcome for survival and growth. In Tom's case it is moral growth, placing the emphasis firmly upon his individual decisions. Charles Kingsley was strongly in favour of the responsibility for moral action being placed upon the individual, a position which was in accord with his religious and social views. He was, for example, against the police being given greater powers, arguing that should this ensue, the

populace would no longer need to act in a morally responsible fash-
ion for responsibility would be taken away from them. Note the
seemingly strange representation of police power as symbolised by
the punitive truncheons guarding Grimes in the asylum scenes.
As the truncheon states: 'he [Grimes] has come to the place where
everybody must help themselves' (Kingsley 1995: 175). Grimes is
the exemplar of the adult who has refused to exercise any social moral
judgement. His punishment is to be placed in a surreal asylum akin
to Hades. Tom, the child, has the chance of learning better.

There are two paths of learning for Tom as a water-baby. The
first is in the immersion in the natural world, and the second is in
the engagement with a quest. It is pertinent that Tom should learn
from nature, rather than the society of man, since mankind has
failed him. Furthermore Kingsley was a very keen naturalist and
fisherman. The fairy-tale narrative abounds with detailed observations of marine life interwoven into scenarios which involve Tom
in various learning experiences. Some are to do with learning about
the behaviour of marine animals, such as the sea anemones; others
are focused upon Tom's behaviour as he discovers how to play;
whilst others are concerned with his moral education. Initially his
form of playfulness is mischievous and destructive. Again Kingsley
uses these passages to emphasise individual responsibility. The
water-fairies are forbidden to intervene. Although they longed to
'teach him to be good', 'Tom had to learn his lesson for himself by
sound and sharp experience' (Kingsley 1995: 51).

The result of his wilfulness is that he unpicks the caddis chrysalis,
and kills her. His reaction is to feel deep shame, although at this
stage he will not admit that he was wrong, but 'felt all the naugh-
tier' (Kingsley 1995: 52). He continues on his rampage until he
meets an 'ugly dirty creature' (Kingsley 1995: 52) which is, unbe-
known to Tom, a dragonfly about to split out of the chrysalis, and
change into the wondrously beautiful adult insect who befriends
him. Kingsley combines Tom's moral lesson with teaching him
about the process of evolution, as the pupa turns into an adult.
Tom himself is making such changes. Whereas the dragonfly is
involved in its own quest for adulthood in a physical sense, Tom's
quest is a moral testing.

Kingsley moves Tom through the underwater world closer and
closer to the challenge of finding Mr Grimes, and in effect, saving
him. The narrative structure of the fairy tale is akin to a surreal stream
of consciousness; the consciousness being that of Kingsley, and the

experience being that of Tom, as he swims through life. Hence the episodes on Tom's journey are surrounded by Kingsley's narrative diversions where he takes the opportunity to debate or satirise numerous contemporary ideas which engaged him, such as whether there was an area of the human brain, the hippocamus minor, which defined the difference between man and ape (Kingsley 1995: 216).

Whereas Tom's quest centres on finding Grimes at the Other-end-of-Nowhere, a place which is set in Eternity, Kingsley's quest centres on the question of Creation. On this convoluted journey the narrative structure, and Tom's journey, become ever more surreal. Islands akin to those created by Swift in *Gulliver's Travels*, and places of moral significance echoing Christian's journey in Bunyan's *Pilgrim's Progress*, are combined with passages which enable Kingsley the satirist to have voice. As Kingsley comes closer to the crux of his text, which is the tension between Darwinism and the existence of God, so any conventional narrative structure becomes inadequate. It is as though Kingsley is searching through confusion; looking for one answer after another. For example, Tom meets with Mother Carey in Peacepool where she makes children 'out of the sea-water all day long' (Kingsley 1995: 148). This is a quasi-scientific model based on the concept of life being initially 'made' in the sea. Kingsley combines the idea of 'making' with manufacture but his expectation is disrupted, for the creative image he sees is that of the Romantic artist who creates from contemplation and imagination:

> He expected . . . to find her snipping, piecing, fitting . . . as men do when they go to work to make anything. But instead of that, she sat quite still . . . looking down into the sea with two great grand blue eyes, as blue as the sea itself.
>
> (Kingsley 1995: 148)

However, the model is still insufficient for Kingsley, for he moves Tom onward to a further contemplation of Creation:

> Then he came to a very quiet place, called Leave-heavenalone. And there the sun was drawing water out of the sea to make steam-threads, and the wind was twisting them up to make cloud-patterns. . . . So the sun span and the wind wove, and all went well with the great steam-loom; as is likely, considering − and considering − and considering −
>
> (Kingsley 1995: 171)

This passage encapsulates the crux of Kingsley's anxiety, that is, how to reconcile his acceptance of Darwinian theory and contemporary scientific theories of creation with his religious views. Kingsley's vision of creation is lyrically recounted in the symbiotic process of sun and sea; the sentence is unfinished for the narrator/ Kingsley is still 'considering –'. Nowhere does God figure in this Creation scene. This is an absence which indicates a serious crisis of faith in Kingsley, a Christian minister. Indicatively Kingsley could neither place nor deny God as his answer, so the sentence remains unfinished.

Significantly, from here the style of the text changes abruptly. Kingsley abandons any further pondering, and produces a disguised gap in the narrative with the phrase: 'And at last after innumerable adventures'. After this hiatus Tom rescues Grimes by enabling him to repent of his crimes. Tom is finally returned to his world by the Irish fairy who takes Tom 'up the backstairs' through the place of absolute knowledge, of which he must remain ignorant, so she blindfolds him. As Kingsley denies Tom of absolute knowledge, so he denies himself. From here on the text moves toward controlled closure; the fantasy world retracts into Tom's reunification with Ellie, and Kingsley returns to the realist frame. Kingsley also maintained a social reality in this reunion, for he does not allow his working class protagonist to marry a child of the landed gentry, for that only happens, as he points out, in fairy tales.

The conclusion of the text is presented as a moral coda, but one where Kingsley playfully absolves himself of the responsibility of having really committed himself to anything. He begins with: 'And now, my dear little man, what should we learn from this parable?' (Kingsley 1995: 183), and concludes with: 'But remember . . . this is all a fairy tale, and only fun and pretence; and, therefore, you are not to believe a word of it, even if it is true' (Kingsley 1995: 184).

Kingsley could not solve the philosophical puzzles which will persist for all time, he could merely engage in an act of contemplation through fantasy. The narrative structure defies simple resolution, for these were not simple problems. Kingsley was confronting the greatest enigma of all, which is the search for the source of Creation: does it lie through science or God? His answer was to pursue his quest through a fairy tale for children.

Chapter 6

Alice as subject in the logic of Wonderland

Lewis Carroll's *Alice in Wonderland*, written in 1864, is one of the seminal texts of fantasy literature for children, falling into the genre of nonsense writing. The mid-nineteenth-century period was one of exploration and rationalisation. It was also the period of classic realism in writing for adults, with George Eliot's *Middlemarch* (1871) representing the height of the form. Against this background *Alice in Wonderland* can be displaced as an irrational and illogical work of surreal fantasy. However, in this essay I contend that Carroll employs a particular logical strategy to explore the nature of human experience by setting Alice on a journey of self-discovery. By logically disrupting certain givens, such as time, place and the meaning of language, Carroll challenges and explores the rational hypotheses upon which the construction of the self was based. Against one context of rationalisation and the systematisation of life, for example, in the spreading influence of railway travel, it was those seeming certainties which were also being disrupted as communication and travel were speeding up; the knowledge base was expanding rapidly, and scientific exploration was challenging the known world. Carroll's surreal fantasy logically endeavours to explore this illogical tension.

In this fantasy world language is a site of contest and not even the physical body is a stable entity. Not surprisingly, Alice becomes a dislocated and confused subject when she enters Carroll's domain.

Carroll frames Alice's fantastic adventures with the idyllic image of a known reality. Alice sits on the bank next to her sister who is reading. Alice is bored by the book in which there are 'no pictures or conversations' (Carroll 1992: 7). The combination of boredom and the heat of the day make her 'feel very sleepy and stupid'. As a result Alice is unprepared for the challenges to come in the world underground. Her intellectual reactions are already slowing down, for when she sees the White Rabbit on the bank it is only on reflection that she thinks it odd that a rabbit should be talking.

In the opening paragraphs the constants of place and time are changing. Although Alice still has a strong sense of self, she cannot control her circumstances and consequently falls down the rabbit hole: 'Alice had not a moment to think about stopping herself before she found herself falling down what seemed to be a very deep well' (Carroll 1992: 8). Her world is becoming physically unpredictable: what she had thought was a rabbit hole might be a well instead. The quality of time is also changing, slowing down so that she can look about her and 'wonder what was going to happen next' (Carroll 1992: 8). Even before her fall is over she is losing her cognitive grasp of the situation. Alice is now 'wondering'; she is engaged in a slow process of consideration, without having sufficient knowledge to predict confidently what *will* happen next. She can, however, forecast that those at home will think her brave since she rationally assesses the fall as being worse than tumbling downstairs. At this stage in her experience she still works on memory and association. She can recall those at home, and anticipate their reaction. As Alice falls she attempts to identify where she is: 'I must be getting somewhere near the centre of the earth' (Carroll 1992: 8).

She continues with her sensible hypothesis based on what she has been taught in the schoolroom:

> 'I wonder what Latitude or Longitude I've got to?' (Alice had not the slightest idea what Latitude was, or Longitude either, but she thought they were nice grand words to say).
>
> (Carroll 1992: 8)

As the narrator points out, although Alice knows the words Latitude and Longitude, she does not understand their meaning. The 'knowledge' provided by her education is inadequate. Carroll is suggesting that Victorian schooling, with its emphasis on rote learning, has not provided Alice with the understanding required to deal with her situation. In this new world the meaninglessness of Longitude and Latitude is more apparent; consequently Alice enters into her own whimsical conjecture. She wonders if she will enter a world which is upside-down, and then mistakenly names her landing place as the 'antipathies' rather than the Antipodes. Alice has innocently identified one of the attributes of the underground world, which is that it will produce experiences which are contrary, and therefore 'antipathetic', to her expectations. Alice is not sure whether she will land in New Zealand or Australia, and so decides to make polite enquiry of whomsoever she might meet. Her manner reflects the codes of Victorian middle-class behaviour into which she has been socialised. In anticipation Alice tries to practise her behaviour by curtseying, but this is impossible since she is falling through mid-air. What Alice discovers is that her course of action is inappropriate. The manners she has learnt are inapplicable to her needs in this world, a discovery to be reinforced as she wanders through Wonderland. Her final ploy is to look for a written sign for the information she requires. By the time Alice lands she has explored the strategies open to her, and also contemplated the constructs of time, place, language and subjectivity which Carroll controls in order to produce the dislocation of Alice as a subject.

Carroll sets rationalism against the unpredictability of fantasy. Alice is attempting to apply rational analysis, drawn from her experience in the world above, to fantastic situations extant in Carroll's world underground. There is a mismatch between the rules which govern the disparate locations – consequently Alice cannot predict what will happen. The unpredictability of her circumstances applies as much to events as it does to her physical state. There is, however, a constant, and that is Alice's desire to enter the garden. Although she eventually finds the key to the garden door, her task is to discover the key to her own physicality in order to enter this image of Eden. She has to become physically attuned to her new environment. She therefore looks to the drink on the glass table as the answer to her problem. Alice has, unfortunately, left the key on the table and is now too small to reach it. Had she predicted that she would be unable to reach the key, the rational action would have been to have held it in her hand, but she has not. As a result she is frustrated by the gap between desire and practicality caused by the failure of her rational capability. Caught in this dilemma Alice begins to divide as a subject. She can no longer confidently project what her physical form will be, and finds herself in such a state of self-conflict that she attempts to box her own ears. Her linguistic confidence is also beginning to drift away, for she 'quite forgot how to speak good English' (Carroll 1992: 13). Memory and association are untrustworthy in this disrupted world. Carroll is employing a reversal of the constructs of self identified by John

Locke in *An Essay Concerning Human Understanding* (1690), that is 'From Experience . . . all our Knowledge is founded.' Alice's experience from the world above is redundant; she therefore descends into a state akin to amnesia, asking herself 'Who in the world am I? Ah *that's* the great puzzle!' (Carroll 1992: 15). The puzzle will not be solved until she has sufficient experience underground. The relationships between experience, memory association and knowledge will then be instituted within the context of the underground world, and Alice will be able to reconstruct herself. However, Alice must undergo a long and perplexing learning process before she can become 'herself' again.

Caught in the frustration of losing her identity she weeps a pool of tears, which later threatens to drown a diminutive version of herself. She is immersed in the product of her own physicality. At this stage she still has the dear memory of Dinah, her cat in the world above. Here, however, Dinah is a threat to the animals with whom Alice communes in the Caucus Race. Furthermore, unless Dinah should also appear in miniaturised form, Alice would be in as great a danger as the mouse. Alice is trying to comfort herself by holding onto a remembered reality: unfortunately, in her present circumstances the recollection is inappropriate. 'Reality' and fantasy are thereby set in conflict, with Alice's identity caught in the middle.

Her sense of self is further dissolved during her exchanges with the Caterpillar which constitute a series of challenges to Alice's identity: 'Who are *you?*' said the Caterpillar (Carroll 1992: 35). Alice's confused and broken reply is:

> 'I – I hardly know, Sir, just at present – at least I know who I was when I got up this morning, but I think I must have changed several times since then.'
>
> (Carroll 1992: 35)

Carroll is moving from an exterior to an interior disruption of Alice's sense of self. Here Carroll focuses upon Alice's diminishing sense of identity through her loss of control over her memory combined with her physically unstable state. For the Caterpillar, changing out of all recognition of himself is a natural and necessary part of his evolutionary cycle. Similar circumstances throw Alice into a state of confusion, for they are different beings. The only way Alice can move on toward achieving her desired entry into the garden is to learn from the Caterpillar, whilst also

recognising their differences. She therefore takes his advice and
eats from the mushroom in order to change her size. The result is
a transformation where she is given new physical proportions.
Despite being physically dislocated out of all self-knowledge Alice
finds that her new form has a satisfying flexibility:

> As there seemed to be no chance of getting her hands up to
> her head, she tried to get her head down to *them*, and was
> delighted to find that her neck would bend about easily in any
> direction, like a serpent.
>
> (Carroll 1992: 42)

Alice is now both a girl-child and a serpent. She is the figure of the
tempter in the Garden of Eden who stands accused by a pigeon, a
fractious cousin to the dove which symbolises peace and gentleness.

> 'Serpent!' screamed the Pigeon . . .
> 'But I'm not a serpent, I tell you!' said Alice. 'I'm a – I'm a'
> 'Well! What are you?' said the Pigeon. 'I can see you're
> trying to invent something.'
> 'I'm a little girl,' said Alice, rather doubtfully, as she remem-
> bered the number of changes she had gone through that day.
>
> (Carroll 1992: 43)

The pigeon employs a false logic and fixes Alice as a serpent. Alice's
sense of identity is thus further confused.

> 'I've seen a good many little girls in my time, but I've never
> seen one with a neck such as that! No, no! You're a serpent;
> and there's no use denying it. I suppose you'll be telling me
> next that you never tasted an egg!'
> 'I have tasted eggs, certainly', said Alice, who was a very
> truthful child.
>
> (Carroll 1992: 43)

Alice provides her own condemning evidence by accepting the
pigeon's false syllogism. Physically and in dietary habit, she is
serpent-like, but not a serpent. Alice is trapped into admitting that
she is both feminine and serpent: tempted and tempter: both the
victim of the Fall and the reason for eviction from Eden. Alice's
innocent desire to enter the garden is set against the context of

Eve's desire which caused her to be ejected from Eden. The confrontation with the pigeon forces Alice into stating that her identity is paramount when the pigeon remarks '". . . and what does it matter to me whether you're a little girl or a serpent?" "It matters a good deal to *me*," said Alice hastily' (Carroll 1992: 43).

This assertive statement is central to Alice's future re-entry into her own world. From this point there is more positive support for Alice, for she begins to meet the characters who will return following her entry into the garden. Prior to this the White Rabbit was her only constant. The Cheshire Cat, a fantastically disembodied version of Dinah, enters the scene. The Cheshire Cat is her only friend in this predominantly confusing and hostile world. It is the only character who refers to an event which is to happen in the future, that is, the game of croquet with the Queen. The Cat's reference gives Alice a sense of location in the future, an event for which she can in some way be prepared. However, her trials are not yet over, for she must engage in the Mad Hatter's Tea-Party. The Cheshire Cat's directions emphasise the diminished importance of time and place in relation to the state of the self, for whichever direction she takes, either toward the Hatter or the Hare, Alice will encounter madness. As it is, both the Hatter and the March Hare are at the tea-party.

The conventions of the Victorian tea-party would have been well-known to Alice as a middle-class child. She therefore acts confidently, since she think she knows how to behave and what should happen. Ironically Alice's attitude contributes to the contravention of those very codes of etiquette which Alice defends, for the party is a scene of social mayhem. The behaviour is unacceptable and the conversation is ruled by rudeness and riddle. This is a place of madness where conversation operates upon flawed logic. The Hatter, for example, confronts Alice with the riddle, 'Why is a raven like a writing desk?' (Carroll 1992: 55). The key to answering a riddle is in the employment of a process of association. Alice cannot answer the riddle because she can remember very little about either ravens or writing desks. Later in the party Alice poses an equally perplexing problem when she asks the Hatter and Hare what they will do when they have used up all the places at the tea table and come back to the beginning. At this point their chain of association will be lost, since time stands still at the party. They have no time to wash the dishes, and consequently, they are unable to change their physical circumstances. The result will be a confusion between taking tea, and having had tea, since there is no time in which to register the difference. The Hatter cannot answer because he cannot predict how to alter the situation. His relationship between experience and memory will always produce the same answer, 'Having tea' and yet not solve the problem of the social convention of requiring a clean place. The Hatter, Hare and Dormouse will continue to circulate upon a spiral of meaninglessness which compounds their insanity. Alice, however, has gained a position of power, for she has posed them the unanswerable question. She is the only one who can make a decision, which is never to go there again. Finally Alice is sufficiently knowledgeable and self-confident to enter the garden where she recognises that she will 'manage better this time' (Carroll 1992: 61).

The garden is not, however, a haven of peace. Alice needs to be self-assured to defend herself against the Queen's threats of decapitation. She gives a polite and confident reply to the impatient and aggressive Queen and has no need to be afraid since she has maintained her sense of self in the place of absolute madness, and can thus ignore the Queen's insane and threatening outbursts. Her protection is her integrity: the unity between self and behaviour. Her experience is now an aid rather than a disability, as she meets familiar and new characters.

Significantly Alice is given explanations about how this world operates. The Mock Turtle and the Gryphon carefully explain the system of education, pointing out the comparison with Alice's own experience in the world above. A relationship between the two worlds is established with Alice as the intermediary maker of meaning. She no longer has to question who she is, and can therefore assertively employ her logic in the court room. Not even the tyrant Queen can conquer her, for Alice defies the regal command to be silent. Alice states that there is no meaning in the rhyme given as the most important piece of evidence. Alice's quest for understanding in this alternative world culminates in the recognition that there is 'no meaning'. In his nonsense text Carroll's application of logical principles has produced a seemingly illogical world. The 'nonsense' in this text is the statement that there is no sense to this trial of life dreamt by Alice. Knowing now who she is, the full-size Alice can collapse the dream world, returning herself to the reality of the bank next to her sister. Alice is back in the locations of real time and place. The certainties by which subjectivity is constructed have been restored, whilst Carroll rules as the master logician in his domain of nonsense.

Section III

The *fin de siècle*

Chapter 7

Testing boundaries

The transition from the nineteenth-century tradition of realism to the innovations of Modernism can be seen as a reaction against one dominant form of expression with a radical reformulation of the concerns of literature. However, in recent times, literary historians have claimed the turn of the century as a distinct literary period with cultural and aesthetic concerns of its own. Rather than merely a point of smooth transition, the *fin de siècle* can be seen as a period characterised by disruptions and conflicts that had been building up throughout the late nineteenth century and were, to some extent, to spur radical experimentation in art with the advent of Modernism. The significance for an understanding of the ways in which children's literature articulates change is manifold during such a period of uncertainty: in particular, contemporary cultural critics consider the *fin de siècle* period to be a 'defining moment for observing the processes by which the boundaries between high culture and popular culture are established and policed' (Pykett 1996: 4).

The dominant view of children's literature as popular culture indicates the need to investigate the form in relation to these processes. While it might be supposed that the aesthetic concerns of the time cannot be found in children's literature, the frequency with which writers of 'literature' as high culture displayed a fascination with the idea of childhood must be acknowledged. Such an interest can be seen particularly in relation to sexuality and the shifting power relationships between men and women at the turn of the century contributing to the tome of children's literature.

A growing cultural divide between masculine pursuits in the city and a concern with commerce, and the shifting status of women within the domestic sphere is sometimes articulated in the literature, raising questions about the role of the feminine during childhood and displaying 'a rejection of qualities associated with femininity' (Nelson 1989: 545). The degree to which male authors, in particular, displayed their fascination with childhood at the turn of the century is, perhaps, an indication of the ways in which shifting gender roles threatened perceived certainties both of an earlier era and of a period prior to adult experience.

In *Children's Literature of the 1890s and the 1990s* (1994), Reynolds refers to the ambivalence of feelings about childhood during this period and locates trends that mark the *fin de siècle* in general terms in the work of authors writing for children such as Oscar Wilde, Kenneth Grahame and J.M. Barrie. These British writers typify a kind of children's fiction that transcends the boundaries of the form and calls attention to the act of writing for children. Although many children's writers earlier in the nineteenth century were to address both adults and children in their fiction, these writers express adult ideas in a different way. Rather than attempting to answer a need to return to the childlike in the adult, many of the texts during the *fin de siècle* address a darker, more pessimistic sensibility.

As a transitional period between the traditions of fantasy writing in the nineteenth century and Modernism at the beginning of the twentieth century, the *fin de siècle* was characterised by uncertainty, both in terms of a reconsideration of the past and an apprehensive approach to the future. The mood in Britain, at least, was characterised by 'society in turmoil. The Boer War exposed cracks in the empire, as the British public encountered ominous signs of social and cultural transformation at home' (Manos and Rochelson 1999: x).

In America, too, the increase in wealth, the precipitate growth of cities and the effects of urban poverty reflected in the fiction of Stephen Crane's *Maggie: A Girl of the Streets* (1893) at the end of the nineteenth century contributed to a sense of both excitement and doubt. The transformation of the country from a rural to an urban culture had implications for the association of children and nature, for there was little place in the cities for children. The changing role of women, too, influenced the literature of the time and the challenges of the first wave of feminism created a general sense of unease. An iconic text of the period, *The Awakening* (1899), by Kate Chopin, centres around the tension between the masculine world, in which women are perceived as man's property (or alone), and the modern world on the horizon, where gender does not hinder self-expression. The struggle of the heroine, Edna Pontellier, centres on her inability to sacrifice her 'self' for her children. It is this fear of the consequences of the liberation of women from family responsibilities which contributed to the uneasiness of the time.

Children, as representatives of the past and as visible embodiments of the future, took on a strong emblematic value at the turn of the century. The growing awareness of the importance of childhood to the adult consciousness was influenced by shifting power structures surrounding gender and sexuality. The radical rethinking required in reaction to Freud's theories of child sexuality, and the fetishising of childhood through the use of children's bodies in art during this period, is also reflected in both adult's and children's literature. Numerous texts reflect a knowingness on the part of children, and an adult gaze that problematises the image of innocence, indicating an uneasiness of expression. While Anita Moss claims that the 'Romantic child had become escapist and regressive' (1991: 226), I would suggest that this was often a result of the increasing difficulty of speaking to or on behalf of children. The ability to believe in 'the child' as a redemptive influence, reminiscent of the novels of Dickens and the high fantasies of the Victorian era, is disrupted by the notion of childhood offered by the theories of Freud, which assign the neuroses of adulthood to childhood experience. While some may claim that Barrie's *Peter and Wendy* (1911) or A.A. Milne's 'Christopher Robin' stories sentimentalise childhood and portray it as an escape from adult consciousness, these texts also demonstrate the problems of performing an adult function: projecting possible worlds into which to grow, and possible selves to become.

Insights into the adult psyche and the importance of one's child-life to one's adult well-being increase this tension. Notions of the innate sexuality and desire in the relationship between parent and child at the heart of Freudian theory, threaten to disrupt Romantic images of innocence and purity. Deep knowledge, once spiritual, once innocent, is imbued with a more threatening knowledge.

A combination of fear and fascination at the rise of the New Woman and homosexuality was expressed in the literature of the period in a fascination with the Gothic, the sensational and the decadent. Bram Stoker's *Dracula* (1897), according to feminist critics (Showalter 1996: 172), provides a subtext of pathological sexuality in its characterisation of vampiric and, thus, devouring, women. Other influential texts of the period express anxiety about an apocalyptic future through a focus on the supernatural, or a misuse of science. Stevenson's *Dr Jekyll and Mr Hyde* (1886), Wilde's *The Picture of Dorian Gray* (1890) and Wells' *The Time Machine* (1890) suggest in different ways a sense of unease, by juxtaposing the notion of the possibilities of savagery beneath the 'normal' exterior of character. In *The Time Machine* in particular, the childlike and apparently innocent Eloi are set in opposition to the dark and threatening Morlocks, who may only live underground. The implication that the human race will, in the future, split into these two factions, can be seen as a reading of the psychopathology of *fin de siècle* life. Though not concerned with children, these texts reflect a mood of uncertainty that is also available in the shifts in tone when addressing children through fiction.

Issues surrounding sexuality find their way into fantasy literature intended for, at least in part, a child audience. Claudia Nelson's discussion of fairy tales of the period focuses on the extent to which authors engage with such issues.

> While they displace their material into apparently traditional fairylands distanced by geography, time and magic from prosaic England, the authors . . . [m]ake startlingly 'adult' use of social questions ranging from the nature of the New Woman and the New Man to homosexuality to the need to contain the male sex drive.
>
> (1994: 88)

Oscar Wilde, in particular, according to Nelson, provides coded and ambiguous messages, at times recalling the use of feminised male characters to embody spiritual goodness familiar to readers of earlier fantasy literature. Originally written for his sons, but finding a fundamentally adult audience, Wilde's stories hint at more complex messages in fairy tales. Redemptive youth is portrayed in sexualised terms and the emphasis on beauty can also be read as a coded discussion of love between men. According to Zipes (1999), his stories 'can be regarded as artistic endeavors on the part of Wilde to confront what he already foresaw as the impending tragedy of his life' (1999: 137). What is more marked, however, in Wilde's work, as in the work of many of the writers of the period, is the performative quality of the narrative.

Although often written for individual children, as was the case in the work of Kingsley, Ruskin and Carroll, these later works provide an adult voice which is too knowing – too aware of itself 'talking to children'. Though Wilde comes closest to echoing the moralising tone of earlier fairy stories, the spiritual messages encompass only one layer of his work. Rather than suggesting the voice of authority, Wilde's narrator presents an ironic view of the world and an arch fatalism, familiar in his plays and poetry for adults. Although he doesn't go as far as the decadent self-parody that characterised the tone of so much literature of the period, the narrative intrusion and the florid descriptions add a decadent quality to the work.

> 'When I was alive and had a human heart,' answered the statue, 'I did not know what tears were, for I lived in the Palace of Sans-Souci, where sorrow is not allowed to enter. In the daytime I played with my companions in the garden, and in the evening I led the dance in the Great Hall. Round the garden ran a very lofty wall, but I never cared to ask what lay beyond it, everything about me was so beautiful. My courtiers called me the Happy Prince, and happy indeed I was, if pleasure be happiness. So I lived, and so I died. And now that I am dead they have set me up here so high that I can see all the ugliness and all the misery of my city, and though my heart is made of lead yet I cannot chose but weep.'
>
> 'What! is he not solid gold?' said the Swallow to himself. He was too polite to make any personal remarks out loud.
>
> (Wilde, 'The Happy Prince': 1)

The emphasis in the story is on the ugliness beneath the surface of beauty and on the notion of sacrifice for love, but Wilde also offers numerous asides about human behaviour, often mocking and satirical, that call attention to his role as moraliser.

The tone of the *Just So Stories* (1983) also suggests an underlying sense of disingenuousness in the direct address in Kipling's repetitive use of 'So that was all right, Best Beloved' and 'Do you see?'. Although Hunt claims that they are '[h]ighly personal, immediate, and whimsical . . . full of family dialect' (Hunt 1994: 101), there is a difference between this whimsy and the familiar asides of a writer like Carroll. There is a sense of playing at a confident voice in the reiteration of such phrases as: 'this is the way the world is' or 'so now you see, Best Beloved'. Within this kind of narrative, however, there is also a sense of the fickleness of humanity and the harshness of lessons to be learned in the journey to adulthood. Similarly, in *The Jungle Book* (1894), the necessity of Mowgli's departure from the jungle into civilisation is double-voiced: it is a necessity, but it is also an inevitable loss. Kipling's own anxieties about British colonialism are also reflected in his portrayal of the cooperation within the animal community, in contrast to the superstition and intolerance in the human world.

Frequently in this period, the deliberate and self-conscious narrative voice imbues such works with an underlying sense of irony that contributes to their interest to an adult audience. Grahame's *The Wind in the Willows* (1908), the numerous versions of Barrie's Peter Pan stories and, to some extent, A.A. Milne's work speak more strongly to the adult reader who can read the text on many levels, and this explains the popularity of such texts among adult audiences. These books are, I would suggest, self-consciously *about* writing for children, rather than merely stories for children. These authors, in particular, offer narrators who address a knowing implied reader – one who may share the sense of insufficiency of the expected role of author as adult authority. The way in which Milne, for example, plays with the storytelling voice in the opening story of *Winnie-the-Pooh* delivers both a narrator for children, and another narrator, playing that part (Hunt 1994). Even his own favourite, *Once on a time . . .*, began as a fairy story for adults, but as Milne himself wrote, 'But as you can see, I am still finding it difficult to explain what sort of book it is. Perhaps no explanation is necessary. Read in it what you like; read it to whomever you like' (1962: vii).

Even Edith Nesbit, who may be considered to address a child audience more exclusively, uses narrative intrusion to call attention to the task of writing children's fiction in a knowing and sometimes satirical way. Authorial interjection and frequent reference to the conventions of writing for children mark a change to the relationship between author and reader which diffuses the power of the author and welcomes the reader in. The opening of *The Story of the Amulet* (1905), for instance, begins with reference to an earlier work in a dismissive way.

> The book about all this is called *Five Children and It*, and it ends up in almost tiresome way by saying –
> 'The children *did* see the Psammead again, but it was not in the sandpit; it was – but I must say no more –'

The reason that nothing more could be said was that I had not then been able to find out exactly when and where the children met the Psammead again.

(Nesbit 1973: 12)

Using the voice of one of the child characters in *The Story of Treasure Seekers* complicates first-person narrative by making it a mystery (though not too much of a mystery) about which character is telling the story. Nesbit is able, at once, to mock the conventions of the domestic tale and adventure story, but also to undermine, though gently, the whole project of authorship.

By calling attention to the storytelling process in this way, Nesbit reveals a self-consciousness in her role as author that is evident throughout the period and becomes even more marked as the forces of Modernist thought take stronger hold in the twentieth century. In some ways, although she could also be considered as an heir to the Romantic tradition in terms of her nostalgia for the past (Moss 1991: 226), she also prefigures postmodernist disruption of narrative evident in the most contemporary texts. Yet Nesbit offers a clearer and more optimistic view of the possibilities for change and renewal than many of the more renowned male authors of the day; those writers who write deliberately for an adult audience. Reynolds (1994) suggests that this may be due to some extent to the resentment on the part of several authors about the popularity of their children's fiction at the expense of recognition of their writing for adults. Though this may be so, it is also an indication of the discomfort and uncertainty in the confident adult author speaking to the 'innocent' child reader.

Some of this discomfort arises from the shifting gender roles at the turn of the century, and it might be suggested that there is a dividing line between the female and male writers of the day in terms of narrative address. Certainly Frances Hodgson Burnett, discussed in more detail in Chapter Nine, in her later writing, shares many of the concerns of writers such as Grahame, yet is much more direct and similar to Nesbit in her approach to children as audience. Burnett's use of the iconic Romantic child, such as Cedric in *Little Lord Fauntleroy* (1885), or Dickon in *The Secret Garden* (1911), appears to hark back to an earlier period. However, her use of nature and the child-in-nature as somehow transcendent reflects the pseudo-pagan spirituality in much of the fiction of the period. The dissipation of organised Christian religion and a dependence on pagan imagery (such as the figure of Pan) points to the need to offer children as readers a possibility of transcendence, yet both Burnett and Grahame undercut that possibility. Burnett embraces an understanding of psychology and challenges imperialist, male-orientated society by using the garden and the Dickon/Pan figure to suggest a kind of androgyny which emphasises qualities of 'goodness, self-sacrifice and Godliness' (Nelson 1999). The uncomfortable ending, in which Mary becomes a mere bit-player in what was once her narrative, appears to dissipate the redemptive power of the story, although some critics disagree (Hunt 1994).

So, too, Grahame's use of narrative structure in *The Wind in the Willows* separates the rite of passage of Toad and Mole from the lyrical chapters to such an extent that they are frequently removed from modern children's editions. Although he could claim that 'Children are not merely people; they are the only really living people that have been left us in an over-weary world' (in Hamilton 1933) the implied readership for these chapters is clearly different to that invited to enjoy the adventures of the foolish Toad. Hunt suggests that the 'narrative voice and stance is not necessarily coterminus with the episodes' (1994: 97), and I would argue that the feeling of loss that endows the 'lyrical' chapters is also present in Toad's last 'long, long, long sigh'. While the ending of Toad's story can be seen as the success of repression of the wayward child, the tone of the ending invites readers to see, in him, the ultimate dissatisfaction of adult life. 'The Piper at the Gates of Dawn', for instance, while offering a stirring vision of the god, Pan, to Mole and Rat, also articulates the impossibility of holding on to that vision.

> As they stared blankly, in dumb misery deepening as they slowly realized all they had seen and all they had lost, a capricious little breeze, dancing up from the surface of the water, tossed the aspens, shook the dewy moss, and blew lightly and caressingly in their faces, and with its soft touch came instant oblivion. For this is the last best gift that the kindly demigod is careful to bestow on those to whom he has revealed himself in their helping: the gift of forgetfulness. Lest the awful remembrance should remain and grow, and overshadow mirth and pleasure, and the great haunting memory should spoil all the afterlives of little animals helped out of difficulties, in order that they should be happy and light-hearted as before.
>
> (Grahame 1980: 109)

This vision of awe is inflected very differently to that of the world at the back of the North Wind. The need to forget the promise of this redeeming vision in order to survive one's waking life indicates a shift in tone from earlier children's fiction; from idealism to a pragmatic sense of loss. In part it is the task of writing that makes the endurance of loss possible, and Grahame's own awareness of this is reflected in his fiction. Just as Grahame constructed a fictional space 'free from the clash of sex' and distanced from the Wide World (and so an oasis from his middle-class life as a banker), so Rat must settle for scribbling to counteract the pull of the open sea.

J.M. Barrie, too, uses his constructed world of Neverland to express and to dissipate the pain of being unable to return to childhood (Wullschlager 1995), or even to find a happily remembered childhood. Barrie's is perhaps the defining voice of children's literature of the *fin de siècle*, for his ability, within an adventure narrative, to articulate the disruptions of the age. Although the story of Peter Pan can be read as a story about the need to grow up, it is also about the inability to do so. Uneasiness, brought about by a shifting sense of gender, an awareness of the sexuality and cruelty of children, and an ironic view of British 'fair play' indicate the work's significance as an expression of the turmoil of the time.

Barrie's form of address, and the complex layering of the implied readership of *Peter Pan and Wendy* (and other versions) also typifies the central difficulty at the heart of the relationship between adult writer and child reader in children's literature as a whole. Jacqueline Rose's analysis of this problematic relationship in *The Case of Peter Pan* (1994) provided a new way of looking at children's fiction, using Barrie's work as an example. The complexity of the power relations between adults and children expressed in *Peter Pan* indicates to Rose the impossibility of children's literature as an innocent interaction. It is the growing awareness of that impossibility that can be traced through a perspective that places children's texts within the history of author/reader communication.

Rather than merely celebrating childhood and rejecting the adult world, Barrie's ambiguity of tone provides a dark vision of youth and a problematic perspective of motherhood. The seemingly 'adult' tension between Peter and Wendy and his rejection of adult life is centred around the idea of the mother and of women, in general; a view echoed in the female emancipation debates during the *fin de siècle*.

It is the tension over the female essence – what it is and what it does, who is to possess it and who to control it – that is the real woman question for the turn-of-the-century fantasy and fact alike.

(Nelson 1994: 103)

Again, a self-consciousness surrounding the role of telling stories to children informs Barrie's ambiguous view of mother-love, framed by Wendy's version:

> That was the story, and they were as pleased with it as the fair narrator herself. Everything just as it should be, you see. Off we skip like the most heartless things in the world, which is what children are, but so attractive; and we have an entirely selfish time, and then when we have need of special attention we nobly return for it, confident that we shall be rewarded instead of smacked.
>
> So great indeed was their faith in a mother's love that they felt they could afford to be callous for a bit longer.
>
> But there was one there who knew better, and when Wendy finished he uttered a hollow groan.
>
> 'What is it, Peter?' she cried, running to him . . .
>
> 'Wendy, you are wrong about mothers.'
>
> They all gathered round him in affright, so alarming was his agitation; and with a fine candour he told them what he had hitherto concealed.
>
> 'Long ago,' he said, 'I thought like you that my mother would always keep the window open for me, so I stayed away for moons and moons and moons, and then flew back; but the window was barred, for mother had forgotten all about me, and there was another little boy sleeping in my bed.'
>
> (Barrie 1987)

Although it is tempting to ascribe this merely to Barrie's own disturbed childhood and his desire to relieve his mother's suffering at the death of his older brother, the doubt about mother-love marks the children's fiction of the age, particularly in the work of male authors. Similarly, his emphasis on the heartlessness of children, repeated several times in the narrative, reveals a sense of mistrust in an enduring vision of past blessedness which typified earlier children's fiction. The notion of the mother as the centre of a child's experience has changed from the Romantic notion of the sublime maternal figure to a problematic relationship. The disruption of patriarchal certainties at the turn of the century, and the shifts in the power structure between genders, offered a challenge to the expectations of masculinity. The predominance of adventure stories and school stories that dominated the children's book market in the mid-nineteenth century provides a backdrop against which to consider the ways that masculinity can be seen to be questioned in the children's fiction of this period. The figure of Captain Hook, for instance, preoccupied with his mother and 'good form', seems a striking contrast to the pirates of Stevenson's *Treasure Island* or the work of Captain Marryat.

I have suggested that female writers of the period offer a more optimistic view and an easier relationship with authorship. While this may have been due to economic necessity – both Burnett and Nesbit were the primary breadwinners in their families – this may also be due to the rise of the professional women and a new confidence. Nesbit's connection with Fabian socialism is also influential in her portrayals of the working class in various novels, and Burnett uses the secret garden not only as a maternal space, but also as an opportunity for a democratic sharing to develop between classes. It can also be that the less optimistic view is an archetypally British response.

The discussion of *The Secret Garden* in Chapter Nine focuses on the book's engagement with imperialism and the redemptive power of nature. Burnett may express views which are critical of British colonial rule, but she is also different to these authors by virtue of her status as an American author. Certainly American children's fiction of the period appears to have a more celebratory tone and a less ambiguous purpose than much of the British fiction considered here. Burnett's sense of the transcendental (the 'Magic') in nature and the recuperative force of the natural world on her child characters is still in keeping with earlier American ideals. Little Lord Fauntleroy, in addition to being a sentimentalised version of the Romantic child, is also an American, who offers an egalitarian vision of freedom to a stodgy English nobleman (Griswold 1992).

It may be that the sense of progress at the turn of the century in America is less inflected with negative emotion, and certainly the notion of becoming the world's leading industrial nation demanded a children's literature that continued to idealise the child. According to MacLeod, this era was the 'high point in American romanticization of childhood, . . . seeing in children elemental qualities of nature unspoiled' (1994: 117). The emphasis on democratic values and the independent spirit meant that, although mainstream fiction responded less positively to cultural developments, children's writers were able to offer their readers a more positive view of the future. The effects of the Civil War on the national psyche, and the failure of Reconstruction, are reflected in the bitterness of tone in the late work of poets and writers who came to prominence earlier in the century. While Walt Whitman had early embodied the new poet, 'singing the nation', he offered a bleaker interpretation of Gilded Age America (Ruland and Bradbury 1991). The idealism of the earlier nineteenth century became impossible in the face of the power of commerce and the destruction of the natural landscape, through war and industry. Mark Twain, too, disgusted by the outcome of the Civil War, wrote misanthropically about the American people. Coining the term, 'the Gilded Age', Twain revealed the emptiness behind the brilliancy of the new wealth of the nation. At the same time, the attraction of commercial success motivated authors like Twain to entertain the populace. L. Frank Baum, the author of *The Wonderful Wizard of Oz*, discussed in Chapter Eight, was similarly caught up in the ambivalence of the Gilded Age.

Although the frontier had been conquered, the American character, defined by westward expansion, became focused on a new frontier of economic power. The role of children to pursue the American values of wealth and success, as well as to demonstrate the virtues of a democratic society, contributed to a rapidly expanding children's publishing industry as the nineteenth century ended. The tension between high culture and popular culture is particularly evident in this growth, and it may be that children's fiction found a more comfortable home in America, although British children's books continued to be read. The need to promote the future to American children may have protected the American children's author from the sense of doubt more typical of British children's fiction of the time (MacLeod 1994).

In many ways, the subtle difference in tone anticipates a more energetic response to modern developments that were to come with the new century. Although the next section will deal more fully with the reactions to Modernism reflected in children's fiction, it is the time of transition experienced at the turn of the century which gives an indication of the growing distance between adults and children as readers.

Chapter 8

The Wonderful Wizard of Oz

Pleasure without nightmares

L. Frank Baum's first book about the Land of Oz was published at the turn of the twentieth century. Although at first glance a timeless tale of fantasy, *The Wonderful Wizard of Oz* (1900) expresses more about the age, as a period of disruption and uncertainly, than its author, who claimed himself to be nonpolitical, probably intended. Whether or not Baum planted a complex political parable of the failure of populism in the Gilded Age within his tale, it is the book's relationship to those American values of 'home and self-determination' (Lurie 1990) which make it interesting within the context of the *fin de siècle*. What is more, the surface simplicity of the book and its history reveal the changing status of children's literature during that period and places it firmly within the boundaries of the popular, in opposition to the high culture of such literary fairy tales as those of Oscar Wilde, for instance.

Frances Hodgson Burnett, like many of the authors discussed above, was deliberately influenced by the British tradition of children's literature and spoke with a dual address to both adult and child audiences. *The Wonderful Wizard of Oz*, however, is unashamedly aimed at children. The episodic nature of the narrative, the flamboyant use of fantastic characters and magical events seem crafted in a free and careless way, and critics often comment on the poor quality of writing in Baum's work. Certainly, the books do not earn many mentions in critical histories of children's literature.

The fact that there is not much to say about the language in the stories is probably deliberate, however. Baum claimed, in his introduction, that he intended to leave behind the 'old-time fairy tale' which, he implied, was no longer relevant to the children of the twentieth century. Looking to education to provide moral improvement, Baum claimed that stories should only be for enjoyment and so provided something which 'aspires to being a modernized fairy tale, in which the wonderment and joy are retained and the heartache left out' (Baum 1994: 53). This view of children's books, as solely entertainment and pleasure without the 'heartaches and nightmares', provides a contrast to those writers who claim to write for an undetermined audience. Baum appeared to regard writing for children as a less worthy aim than writing for adults. In an inscription to his sister, he wrote:

> When I was young I longed to write a great novel that should win me fame. Now that I am getting old my first book is written to amuse children. For, aside from my evident inability to do anything 'great,' I have learned to regard fame as a will-o-the-wisp which, when caught, is not worth the possession; but to please a child is a sweet and lovely thing that warms one's heart and brings its own reward.
>
> (Gardner and Nye 1994: 42)

While it is ironic that Baum would achieve great fame through his connection with the Oz stories, it is also true that his desire for 'greatness', and its escape from his grasp is written into his tale. The powerful discourses of wealth and fame imprinted on Americans by authors such as Horatio Alger, Jr are called into question in the story of Dorothy's quest for Kansas and her encounters with the Wizard of Oz.

Alger, who died in 1899,

> Produced mass fiction, contributed to popular culture, and came to stand at the margins of respectable literature. Dependent upon the market, the author shaped a product that would be consumed. Alger's own experience pointed out the struggle to define manliness and potency in relationship to production, consumption and class.
>
> (Nackenoff 1997: 75)

Described as one of the most influential American writers of all times, Alger's apparent dedication to the capitalist ethos had an impact on writers like Baum, who aimed to construct a fiction as a product to be consumed. While it is possible to read his work as a celebration of American growth and of capitalism, it can also be read as a text which expresses a yearning for home, the rural and the domestic world of the feminine. Dorothy may be a strong female figure for the period and her journey is a rare example of a heroic quest conducted by a girl (West 1992: 125). She is capable of killing powerful witches and she is a leader of men. The Scarecrow, Tin Woodman and Lion all follow her example in the search for Oz. However, she is a strong female in a male world and she belongs, or certainly *wants* to belong, back in Kansas with her Aunt Em. The opposition of the masculinity of the city and the feminine qualities of the rural are played out again in this story, dissipating the threat of the strong female, just as the sensation fiction of the *fin de siècle* attempted to do through the portrayal of disease and madness (Dowling 1996).

Social upheaval, whether due to female emancipation or the rapid rise of the American city, does not appear directly in Baum's work, although it is known that he had a close affiliation with the suffragette movement (Hearn 1973). Yet there is an undertone in the work that suggests a relationship with Baum's own struggle to fit the description of rags-to-riches, which provides a subtext to the wonder tale. Whether in his career in commerce prior to his authorial success, or in his attempts to capitalise on the popularity of the Oz books with film and theatre adaptations, as well as an early version of merchandising, Baum embraced the notion of American enterprise and commercialisation with zeal. He was, according to his biographers, an 'improvisational entrepreneur' and a 'flamboyant promoter', reminiscent, perhaps, of the Wizard of Oz, revealed finally to be a humbug showman from Nebraska (Nye 1994).

At the same time, however, *The Wonderful Wizard of Oz* offers a more complex, less wholehearted view of the growing success of American society. An ambivalent attitude toward the transformation of life at the turn of the century, and the move away from the rural to the urban, typified much of the literature of the period, and Baum, though living the life promoted by dominant cultural discourses, 'was disturbed by the Gilded Age' (Zipes 1983: 122).

While the fantasy lands that Dorothy encounters in her quest to find Oz and return to Kansas conform to Baum's fairy tale model, filled as they are with witches and talking animals, the sense of a changing American landscape is never far away.

At first glance, it is difficult to understand Dorothy's attachment to Kansas. The prairie is described as grey and an unsuitable environment for a child.

When Aunt Em came there to live she was a young, pretty
wife. The sun and wind had changed her, too. They had taken
the sparkle from her eyes and left them a sober gray; they had
taken the red from her cheeks and lips, and they were gray
also. She was thin and gaunt, and never smiled, now. When
Dorothy, who was an orphan, first came to her, Aunt Em had
been so startled by the child's laughter that she would scream
and press her hand upon her heart whenever Dorothy's merry
voice reached her ears; and she still looked at the little girl
with wonder that she could find anything to laugh at.

(Baum 1994: 55–6)

Compared to the colour of the Emerald City and the liveliness
of the characters encountered in Oz, a desire to return to the prairie
is difficult to understand. The jarring description of Aunt Em's
reaction to Dorothy's laughter is, perhaps, offered as a contrast to
the fantasy that will follow – real life is unsuitable for children.

Following this detailed description, Dorothy's return to Kansas
at the end of the story is only six lines long and lacking in a sense
of physical place. There is no mention of greyness in this passage,
but only action and dialogue. It is Aunt Em's embrace that signifies the return home. The once beautiful woman, 'fold[s] the little
girl in her arms and cover[s] her face with kisses' (Baum 1994:
193) Although Zipes claims that the conclusion signifies that
'Dorothy has a utopian spark in her which should keep her alive
in gray surroundings' (Baum 1994: 128), I would argue that, as in
so many of the children's books discussed, Dorothy's search indicates the desire for the feminine realm that is at the heart of the
uncomfortable position of children's literature, as we head toward
modern times.

While the story structure of home and back again is familiar to
most children's narratives, Baum underplays its importance, prefer-
ring, instead, to place his narrative emphasis on the adventure and
the imaginative power of the Emerald city. It is certainly this aspect
of his work that impresses critics. Seen as a hymn to consumer
culture, or a utopian populist community, the Emerald City is
at the heart of the tension of the book. Torn between support and
subversive criticism of the American Way, Baum's work seems to
'exalt the opulence and magic of the metropolis' (Parker 1994).
Dorothy and her companions are continually 'dazzled by the
brilliancy of the wonderful city' (Baum 1994: 117). The descrip-

tion that follows emphasises both the richness of the city, in its marble and jewels, and its greenness. 'Everyone seemed happy and contented and prosperous' (Baum 1994: 110).

This richness and happiness is based on a false premise, however, and casts doubt on a reading of the Emerald City as a utopia. Upon arriving at the Emerald City, Dorothy and her companions, including Toto, must be locked into green spectacles, for which only the gatekeeper holds the key. He explains that

> If you do not wear spectacles the brightness and glory of the Emerald City would blind you. Even those who live in the city must wear spectacles night and day. They are all locked on, for Oz so ordered it when the City was first built.
>
> (113)

Thus, the brilliancy is false and the meaning of *seemed* in the claim that everyone seemed content takes on a new importance. The sense that the appearance of wealth and success is but an appearance suggests a reading in keeping with the response to the Gilded Age seen in other authors of the day. The Wizard, too, is a humbug. Rather than the terrifying authority ruling over the land, he is only playing with sleight of hand and tricks learned as a man of the circus. When discovered, he reveals the fact that he had merely built the city to 'amuse myself and to keep the people busy' (154), Though he had originally named it the Emerald City because 'the country was so green and beautiful', he made people wear green spectacles to 'make the name fit better'. Although he claims that the people have the 'good things' to keep them happy, this falseness suggests a comment on American consumerism and the uneasy relationship between appearance and 'truth'.

A famous essay by Henry Littlefield, 'The Wizard of Oz: Parable on Populism' (1964), claimed that Baum had intended the Emerald City to stand for Washington, DC and the Wizard, for a president of the Gilded Age. While the nature of the parable is often called into doubt, the criticism of Gilded Age America is certainly marked, as well as Baum's allegiance to populist qualities of heart, mind and self-determination that define the American character. What is more, it is Dorothy, 'the small and meek', who conquers the witches, thereby freeing the Winkies from slavery, and who brings Wisdom, Love and Courage to rule in Oz. For Baum, it seems, it is the ordinary people who are celebrated, rather than the humbugs.

Dorothy's function, to liberate Oz and to bring ordinary virtues to a false world, is facilitated by women. Not only is her love for Aunt Em her motivation to begin her journey, but her actions are affected by the four witches in the land. Both wicked and good witches influence the course of events, while the male figures of the Scarecrow, Tin Woodman and Lion trust the false Wizard to provide them with qualities they already possess. If this is an indication of Baum's opinion of the drive for female emancipation, it is important to note that Dorothy returns to the domestic sphere at the end of the story, and ceases to play a part in the larger world.

As an expression of the uneasiness and anxiety of the *fin de siècle*, *The Wonderful Wizard of Oz* offers conflicting visions of its time. On the one hand, Baum portrays a multifaceted and exciting journey through a fantasy world, narrated as though directly to a child audience. On the other, he offers a subversive challenge to the values of that fantasy world, subtly suggesting a return to an earlier utopian idea of America, based on the land and the self-reliance of its people. The ambivalence of this text in relation to American idealism is transformed in later stories in the series. Zipes notes that as Baum 'became disappointed with the American way of life', Oz finally became home and an exile from America (Zipes 1983: 122). Baum's own conflicts are reflected in his place in the history of children's literature. Freely admitting that he could not approach high art, he chose to write 'only' for children, confirming, for the public, the status of children's literature as popular and unliterary.

Chapter 9

Romanticism vs. Empire in
The Secret Garden

Literary and historical discussion of British imperialism in writing for children from the mid-nineteenth century to the early twentieth century concentrates upon those texts that embody the values conducive to promoting the expansion and support of the empire (see for example Eldridge 1996 and Richards 1989). The focus falls upon the adventure stories for boys and domestic fiction for girls. Adventure stories for boys, typified by Ballantyne's *Coral Island* (1857) and Henty's *Clive of India* (1884) represent models of patriotic, imperialist adventurers, who are certain of their actions, and unquestioning of their values. A similarly pro-imperialist position emerges in the critical discussion of domestic fiction for girls, demonstrating the production of a model of femininity compliant with the values of British imperialism (Richards 1989). The anti-imperialist position, which becomes more evident at the turn of the century, is readily examined by critics through Rudyard Kipling's adventure story, *Kim* (1901), which is set in India under British rule. In the genre of domestic fiction of the *fin de siècle*, Frances Hodgson Burnett is also arguing an anti-imperialist position. Both *The Secret Garden*, published in 1911 and *A Little Princess*, published in 1905, take British imperialism in India as their context.

In *The Secret Garden* Burnett initially positions her protagonist, Mary Lennox, as the innocent victim of British imperialism. She does this by constructing the character and childhood experiences of Mary as negative projections against an idealised model of the Romantic child, which is initially implied, rather than stated in the text. The Romantic child would be expected to have a quality of innocence; to be imaginative and playful, and also to display an intuitive relationship with nature. The embodiment of these abstract aspects would be symbolised by an attractive personality and the physical beauty associated with childhood. Ideally these positive qualities would be nurtured by a loving and caring family which also allowed the freedom for the child to explore physically and intellectually. As a result of Mary's early childhood in India, her character has sadly developed in a contrary way to the suggested ideal model which underpins Burnett's text. Mary is a physically unattractive, lonely and unhappy child who has not known the pleasures of childhood because she has been emotionally neglected by her parents. The reasons for such neglect are directly related to British imperialism in India. Her father, as an administrator of imperialist power, was too involved with the work of British government, or too ill, to have time for his daughter. Her mother was also part of the invasive imperialist machinery of government social life. She was so entranced with the trappings of rule, the Government dinner parties and balls, that she 'had not wanted a little girl at all' (Burnett 1987: 1).

Mary, the unwanted child, is estranged from her parents by the demands and attractions of imperialist rule. Instead of being cared for by her mother, Mary is given over to an Ayah. (An Ayah is an Indian nurse who has the status of a servant.) As a consequence of this denial of parental responsibility, Mary learns to be a ruler, rather than a child. She commands her native servants in an imperious manner, insulting them as she sees fit. Mary has no reason to govern herself, and is therefore emotionally self-indulgent, engaging in self-centred fits of rage. She is also indulged by having servants, consequently she is not required to do anything for herself, not even to dress herself. The circumstances of life under imperialist rule have emphasised the negative and antisocial qualities in Mary, and have prevented her from learning the positive traits which are ideally developed in childhood, such as love, laughter, playfulness and a positive sense of self. She is further 'deskilled' by her early childhood experiences in that she has not learned to take care of herself practically. The circumstances of imperialism have produced a child who is emotionally isolated and yet physically dependent.

The opening Indian section of the novel presents a sad and diseased image of childhood symbolised by the episode of the cholera epidemic which strikes down Mary's parents and her Ayah. The orphaned Mary consequently arrives in England unprepared for the emotional and social expectations of English society. She has been brought up as an 'English' child in India, but this cultural construction is one which is dissociated from the realities of English life. In truth, Mary is neither English, nor Indian, but is caught between two cultures, belonging to neither. Mary has to learn to position herself as an English person living in England. On her arrival in England the weather, the landscape, the Yorkshire dialect and the behaviour expected of an English child within the class system are foreign to her. Burnett uses the Yorkshire moorland in particular, to demonstrate poor Mary's dislocated state of being. What Mary knows is that she is being taken to live in 'a house standing on the edge of a moor' (Burnett 1987: 19); however, she does not know what a moor is, and so asks Mrs Medlock, who answers: 'Look out of the window in about ten minutes and you'll see,' . . . 'You won't see much because it is a dark night, but you can see something' (Burnett 1987: 19).

Mrs Medlock's refusal to explain the meaning of the word 'moor' means that Mary has to learn what it is through her own observations. When they reach the moorland, Mary cannot read the signs she is receiving from this strange environment. Her confusion is both emphasised by, and symbolised by, the darkness of night.

> The carriage lamps shed a yellow light on a rough-looking road which seemed to be cut through bushes and low growing things which ended in the great expanse of dark apparently spread out before and around them. A wind was rising and making a singular, wild, low rushing sound.
>
> 'It's – it's not the sea is it?' said Mary . . .
>
> 'No, not it', answered Mrs Medlock, 'Nor it isn't fields, nor mountains, it's just miles and miles and miles of wild land that nothing grows on but heather and gorse and broom, and nothing lives on but wild ponies and sheep.'
>
> Mary felt as if the drive would never come to an end, and that the wide, bleak moor was a wide expanse of black ocean through which she was passing on a strip of dry land.
>
> (Burnett 1987: 21)

This is a strange world where Mary cannot decipher the information fed to her senses. She is a traveller in a foreign sensory landscape. Intuition will not suffice, for Mary has to learn the language of this unfamiliar landscape. She must learn what the sounds of the wind mean; how to distinguish between land and sea. Burnett ends this episode with the comment 'It was this way Mistress Mary arrived at Misselthwaite Manor, and she had perhaps never felt quite so contrary in all her life' (Burnett 1987: 23).

Caught in this state of conflict which Burnett sums up as being 'contrary', curiosity is Mary's saving attribute. She wants to know; she needs to learn, and is therefore willing to undergo a process of change, even if she is somewhat reluctant at first. Such reluctance is understandable, for there is so much for Mary to learn and assimilate. She has to shed the destructive imperious authority learned in the hierarchical power structures of India under British rule, and learn to be both cooperative and independent. Burnett 're-educates' Mary through the relationship with Martha, the good-natured serving girl, and through her relationship with the landscape of the Yorkshire moors. Martha is a caring person who responds to Mary and tries to understand the poor child's situation, gently leading her out of her state of isolation and confusion. The basis of power relations – ruler over servant – are reversed because it is Martha who has more knowledge, and therefore more 'power' than Mary. Burnett's point here is that Martha is willing to share her knowledge, rather than use it as source of power over the child. On her first morning at Misselthwaite it is Martha who gives Mary information about the nature of the moor, and begins that process of the movement for Mary from ignorance to knowledge; from strangeness to familiarity; from isolation to belonging.

> 'What is that?' she (Mary) said, pointing out of the window . . .
> 'That's the moor,' (said Martha) with a good-natured grin.
> 'Does tha' like it?'
> 'No,' answered Mary. 'I hate it.'
> 'That's because tha'rt not used to it,' . . .
> 'I just love it. It's none bare. It's covered wi' growin' things as smell sweet. It's fair lovely i' spring and summer when th' gorse and broom an' heather's in flower. It smells o' honey an' there's such a lot o' fresh air – an' th' sky looks so high an' th' bees an' skylarks makes such a nice noise hummin' an' singin'. Eh! I wouldn't live away from th' moor for anythin'.'
> (Burnett 1987: 25)

Martha's enthusiastic description of the moor is filled with energy and sensual experience, offering a wholesome and stimulating image to Mary, which puzzles her at first. This initial interaction with Martha fuses together the focal point of Mary's problems inherent from her previous experience in India: the dislocation between self, landscape and society. Martha presents a positive model for Mary, and also offers the lonely child love. From this first positive encounter Mary also learns to recognise and appreciate servants as people. There is a clear parallel drawn here between Martha and the Indian Ayah, as Mary reflects on their differences in behaviour:

> She wondered what this girl (Martha) would do if one slapped her in the face. She was a round, rosy, good-natured looking creature, but she had a sturdy way which made Mistress Mary wonder if she might not slap her back – if the person who slapped her was only a little girl.
>
> (Burnett 1987: 25)

Mary is already beginning to move from the unnatural position of ruler to the natural one of being a child.

With Martha's help, support and love Mary's curiosity about the moorland leads her to a state of enhanced physical well-being. A chain reaction begins; Mary meets Martha's brother, Dickon. Dickon will become her mentor. He is, in many ways, her opposite, for he is the idealised Romantic child: loving and understanding nature; patient and at one with his environment. Through him the seeds of childhood are allowed to grow in Mary as they discover and restore the secret garden together.

The garden, like Mary, is a neglected place; left uncared for, behind the imprisoning walls, it has become a tangle of thorns and briars. Nurture, care and love restore the beauty and freedom of this wilderness. In turn Mary blossoms into a natural and healthy child, and is able to share this healing experience with Colin, her cousin. The critique of imperialism is continued through Mary's relationship with Colin. He also displays the crippling consequences of neglect. Whereas Mary was abandoned for the projected patriotic 'love' of the mother country by the administrators of imperialism, Colin is rejected because of the misplaced love for his mother, who is but a ghost. Both children suffer as orphans of absent mother figures. Colin is imperious in his behaviour, mirroring the self-indulgent and sickly child Mary once was when in India. He is as ignorant of the real world of England beyond the self-elected prison of his bedchamber as Mary was when she first arrived. Burnett's critique of imperialism is continued through her characterisation of Colin. He is described as 'A Young Rajah', commanding attention, and in danger of degenerating even further into physical debilitation by his misplaced judgement, his fears of becoming a hunchback. Through the interaction between Mary and Colin, Burnett makes it clear that she is principally attacking British imperialism and the abuse of power rather than Indian culture. By the time Mary is able to have a positive effect on Colin, she has been through the learning process which has separated out her Indian experience into that which was resultant of the negative power structures of British imperialism, and that which is to be valued in the true culture, i.e. the native culture of India. She can, therefore, identify Colin's misbehaviour as being like a young Rajah, because she understands the destructive use of power:

> 'Once in India I saw a boy who was a Rajah. He spoke to his people just as you spoke to Martha. Everybody had to do everything he told them – in a minute. I think they would have been killed if they hadn't.'
>
> (Burnett 1987: 146)

The Rajah, like the English in India, wields power over the common people. Burnett has developed her political argument, removing imperialism from being solely a phenomenon of Englishness to a form of rule arising in other cultures: the imperialist Indian Rajah rules his fellow Indian. Mary can understand the dangers of Colin's behaviour because she is able to relay it through her knowledge drawn from India. Her early foreign experiences are now working positively because they are set within a framework of understanding. She is no longer the English child from India who has a centre of ignorance. That positive knowledge is also transposed through language, whereas previously her ignorance was realised in language, as in the instance of her first encounter with the moor cited above. Mary can now tell stories about India, which fascinate and calm Colin. Her background of strangeness, of otherness, is now a positive source of knowledge because she can set her 'Indian-ness' against a social and physical context of English reality which she now understands. Colin is able to become a passive adventurer through Mary's stories of the outside world, and to gradually turn to the real adventures of growth which are embodied in the recovery of the secret garden.

Mary's journey of discovery through *The Secret Garden* is one where she will learn to be a child growing through her early damaging experiences. In India her garden could only be a dusty and unsatisfactory foreshadowing of the glorious garden the children will finally enjoy in England, because, like her, it was out of place in that environment. Shakespeare referred to England as 'This royal throne of kings', 'this other Eden'. Frances Hodgson Burnett believed in rescuing Eden from the ravages of imperialism. She produced a fictive trio of children who metaphorically learned to uproot the ravaging weeds of imperialism, prune out social division, and from chaos created harmony: peace in the revisioned Eden. Burnett's achievement is not one of a postcolonial position, for at the turn of the century this was not a viable vision. She does, however, move the consciousness of the coming generation toward a more equitable position of power relationships where the sense of self could be at peace with the landscape, finding a place where they truly belonged. The peace of the garden was no longer an unattainable secret, but a blossoming reality.

Section IV

Modernism

Chapter 10

New voices, new threats

The beginning of the new century and the shifting response to social and cultural change brought about a renewal in children's literature and a change in its circumstances. Presaged by the conflict and confusion which characterised the *fin de siècle*, the separation of child and adult experience and a further expansion in the children's book market, indicated a growing perception of children as 'other'. As the twentieth century progressed, and the fears of apocalypse grew more immediate, the need to offer children optimistic futures was more compelling, but more difficult. This unease, made more complex by the insights into the human mind provided by the increasing prominence of psychoanalytic ideas, made the image of the child more mysterious and threatening. Rather than fearing the sinfulness of children as in the nineteenth century, the twentieth century ended with fear of the actions of the actual child. Children-as-murderers appear to signify a society in its death-throes; always in reference to the image of innocence derived from Romanticism, the evil, out of control child becomes an indication of our own moral poverty and inability to exert influence in the world. Children's literature of the period deals with these fears, either by escaping from them and retreating to a Romantic image of innocence, or by addressing children through fractured narratives.

The rejection of religion, the loss of a 'centre', the fear of a growing rift between culture and populism and the impact of the expansion of the industrial world had an undeniable impact on the adult writers of children's literature. At the same time, the further separation of child and adult markets for fiction had a pragmatic effect on what was produced. At a time when art and literature were experiencing an explosion of innovation in response to the changing world, the majority of children's books seem repetitive and derivative, although there are exceptions.

Given this situation, it may seem strange to refer to Modernist experiment in the same breath as children's books. The early Modernist aesthetic, challenging the already said and rejecting the certainties of bourgeois realism, seems far removed from the popular children's fiction of the early twentieth century. Richmal Crompton's William stories, Arthur Ransome's adventures, the reactionary fiction of Noel Streatfeild or the ubiquity of Enid Blyton suggest that children's literature of the period was self-contained and solidly conventional, yet the age is also marked by a growing consciousness of the importance of childhood articulated in literature for both children and adults. The use of the child as a focalising consciousness in fiction for adults, by, among others, Henry James and D.H. Lawrence, reflected the search for 'self' amidst the alienation of modern living.

Interest in children as representations of pre-social beings suggests a connection with the Modernist fascination with the primitive and the search for origins (Levenson 1999). To writers and thinkers of the early twentieth century, the notion of modernity was double-edged. The power of machines and the excitement of scientific and technological progress were tempered by the loss of human connection and the natural world. The modern world: progress-driven, disrupted by world wars and the threatened destruction of the human race, came to signify the ultimate loss of innocence – a totally adult, grown-up world. The need to find a way to respond, through art, to modernity led to a search to find new ways of saying. The urge to break away from expected ways of seeing and portraying modern experience inevitably led writers and thinkers to look back at childhood for a rejuvenation of the imagination. Childhood offered an escape from the already said, as children were seen to approach experience with an original, naïve way of seeing. Twain's use of Huck as narrator in *The Adventures of Huckleberry Finn* provided a model for the naïve voice as a way of looking at the world in a different, and ironic, way. Admired by Modernists such as Gertrude Stein for the use of childlike vernacular, Twain demonstrated the ways in which Huck's lack of sophistication uncovers the inhumanity of ante-bellum society.

While it was more likely to find texts which sentimentalised the misuse of words and 'babytalk' in order to confirm the innocence of children, the role of language as a socialising and controlling force is central to many of the enduring texts of the early twentieth century.

Though A.A. Milne has more in common with the authors of the *fin de siècle* and some critics, such as Wullschlager (1995), deny any connection between Milne and Modernism, his work helps to describe the subtle transitions between *fin de siècle* writing and the influence of Modernism. His blending of fantasy and reality and his double address to both children and adults is clearly indebted to Kenneth Grahame and J.M. Barrie. In addition, his resentment surrounding his success as a children's writer at the expense of more literary endeavours is a further indication of the tensions surrounding the status of children's literature as anti-literary. His tendency to call attention to the process of storytelling is allied to the archness of tone discussed in Chapter Seven within the context of the *fin de siècle*.

However, the subject of language within both *Winnie-the-Pooh* (1926) and *The House at Pooh Corner* (1928) suggests an awareness of the social power of language, and the different ways in which children use it, that reflects Modernist concerns. The childlike misapprehension of language ('Trespassers Will', the 'expotition' to the North Pole, etc.) and the misuse of grammar and spelling is central to the humour and enduring popularity of Milne's work, particularly for an adult readership.

Milne is clearly writing for the knowing adult as well as for a child readership (Hunt 1994). The running theme about the writing of poetry or 'hums' in the Pooh stories suggests an awareness of the new poetics of Modernism. Eeyore's poem in the closing episode, either a work of free verse or failed attempt at rhyme, may even have been meant as a satirical representation of Modernist attempts.

> I ought
> To begin again,
> But it is easier
> to stop.
> Christopher Robin, good-bye,
> I
> (*Good*)
> I
> And all your friends
> Sends –

I mean all your friend
Send –
(*Very awkward this, it keeps going wrong*)
Well, anyhow, we send
    Our love
END.

(Milne 1979: 164)

The tension between correct grammar and poetic diction is confronted with humour here, but there is also a darker suggestion of the limitations of language 'rules'. It is Christopher Robin's eventual engagement with the symbolic order; his adult knowledge of language and a rejection of his childish ways of communicating that signal his departure from the Hundred Acre Wood. In 'Rabbit's Busy Day', the discovery of what Christopher Robin does in the mornings shows Milne's awareness of the implications of the child's changing relationship to language.

What does Christopher Robin do in the mornings? He learns. He becomes Educated. He instigorates – I *think* that is the word he mentioned, but I may be referring to something else. He instigorates knowledge.

(Milne 1981: 98)

Rabbit refers to Christopher Robin learning to form his letters and spell, but Milne suggests that this is a loss. While

GON OUT
BACKSON
BISY
BACKSON,
    (Milne 1981)

although misunderstood by Rabbit, generates a number of exciting possibilities for adventure, the episode ends with a correctly spelled message, thereby closing off that sense of play of meaning. The final story, though ending with a rather sentimental image, frequently quoted, of Christopher Robin and Pooh 'always playing', suggests that adult language is tired and lacking in imagination, when Pooh states his fear that 'Christopher Robin won't tell me anymore' (1981: 178).

The notion that children may have a different relationship to language – a relationship that suggests a revolutionary attitude to 'conventional' usage – is also familiar in the works of key Modernist writers, such as Gertrude Stein and Virginia Woolf.

At the same time, the frequent use of children as characters in fiction of the period is often considered to be a feature of the effort to find a new perspective on modern experience. 'The Rocking-horse Winner' (1926) by D.H. Lawrence and *What Maisie Knew* (1897) by Henry James are among a number of works that explore the alienation of modern adult life through a naïve child figure. In Lawrence's short story the uncanny is brought into play, as the young boy responds to his family's desire for money, by riding his rocking-horse. He is thus able to predict the winners of horse races. The callousness and greed of the family is contrasted with the trusting nature of the boy, who dies in his pursuit of 'luck'.

In a more complex and difficult narrative, James explores the dawning consciousness of a young child in *What Maisie Knew*. Through the use of a stream of consciousness, James delivers a picture of adult infidelity through the myriad impressions of adult behaviour, seen through uncomprehending eyes. In *The Turn of the Screw* (1898), as well, the naïvety of James's young characters uncovers the sexual secrets hidden within multiple narrative frames.

These children recall the image of the Romantic innocent but this innocence now uncovers a threatening, rather than transcendent, knowledge of the adult world. It is the search for the origins of self that lie behind this dangerous knowledge. The absence of answers in religion and traditional ways of perceiving the self, and the philosophical questioning arising from this absence, contribute to the existential angst, which typifies the intellectual response to modern experience.

The need to create reason for one's existence, rather than to rely on some prior notion of human purpose, energises much of the work of the Modernist period, and disrupts received ideas in often radical ways. A number of writers approach the task of writing for children as an attempt to find a language that rejects the rational and conventional, in order to 'make it new'. Kristeva's notion of Modernist writing as a revolutionary form (cited in Moi, *Sexual/Textual Politics*, 1985) implies a feminine, pre-symbolic quality to the poetry of the period that is also available in some experimental writing for children. Many of these features: the absence of rational narrative, the fluidity and the use of sensual, rhythmic and rhyming language, are familiar to readers of the writing of George MacDonald, discussed in Chapter Four. As I have argued, it is the narrative approach to a particular kind of implied reader, informed by Romantic notions of transcendent understanding, that moves through the history of children's literature. Differently inflected in a modern age, feelings of alienation and loss of self have an impact on what it is possible to offer children, who can no longer be protected from the suffering caused by modern experience.

Again, the American response has a more positive aspect and the Modernist experiment was viewed, from the continent as well, as a reaffirmation of American's characteristic claim to challenge old ways. The freshness of the naïve voice could be seen to celebrate change and renewal, rather than as a reaction against it. D.H. Lawrence, in *Studies in American Literature* (1924), described American literature in terms of its 'childishness', but attributes this to its newness.

> It is hard to hear a new voice, as hard as it is to listen to an unknown language. We just don't listen. There is a new voice in the old American classics. The world has declined to hear it, and has babbled about children's stories.
>
> (Lawrence 1973: 296)

The relationship between the child as a primitive, and the language system, which embodies the social world, is embedded in the project of writing for children. The radical disruption of accepted forms of language is connected with children's natural tendency to disregard or subvert these boundaries. Modernist fascination with the search for forms of expression less constrained by convention characterised artistic achievement, and child language provided possibilities for innovation. Juliet Dusinberre's investigation into the connections between Modernism and children's literature: *Alice to the Lighthouse* (1999), notes that writers of the Modernist period, like Woolf, were influenced by key Victorian texts for children, such as Carroll's fantasies, and awakened to other ways of perceiving self and reality.

However, it is the use of the children's story and attempts to make use of the child's relationship to language in story that suggests this Modernist fascination. Joyce opens *A Portrait of the Artist as a Young Man* (1916) with a conventional fairy-tale beginning, yet adopts the storytelling voice of an adult talking down to a child. At once, Joyce emphasises the importance of child experience in the life of the individual and comments on the process of telling stories 'in a child's voice':

> Once upon a time and a very good time it was there was a moocow coming down along the road and this moocow that was coming down along the road met a nicens little boy named baby tuckoo. . . .
>
> (1972: 7)

This attempt to echo a childlike use of language is meant to shock and defamiliarise the reader's sense of narrative, yet it expresses a great deal about the difference between conventional systems of storytelling and the child-voice. Although not intended for a child audience, Joyce's use of repeated phrases and made-up words has a great deal in common with the stream of consciousness technique found in many Modernist texts. Attempts to break away from the 'already said', and to challenge the ways in which it is possible to convey the thought processes of the human mind, often led Modernist writers to look to more primitive and, thus, less socially controlled forms of communication.

Virginia Woolf's concern with primitive forms of expression is also articulated in *Flush* (1933), told from the point of view of Elizabeth Barrett Browning's dog. Although only marginally a children's book, *Flush* expresses Woolf's fascination for the expressiveness of pre-language, suggesting an allegiance between animals and children. Woolf's own attraction to the 'irreverence' of childhood, and the desire to approach understandings of self beyond language, is conveyed in the relationship between Barrett Browning and her dog.

> Can words say anything? Do not words destroy the symbol that lies beyond the reach of words? She was lying, thinking; she had forgotten Flush altogether, and her thoughts were so sad that the tears fell upon the pillow. Then suddenly a hairy head was pressed against her; large bright eyes shone in hers; and she started. Was it Flush, or was it Pan?
>
> (Woolf 1998: 27)

The poet's desire to attain an understanding beyond words is reflected in her relationship with the lapdog, suggesting a more primitive, yet necessary, perception regarding the artistic process, reflected in the work of other prominent Modernists. Reminiscent of the pastoral chapters of Grahame's *The Wind in the Willows*, Woolf offers a similar sense of the inexpressible nature of the subconscious; a sense that is unreachable by adult consciousness.

Gertrude Stein, too, attempted in her only work of children's fiction to capture the child's voice in narrative. *The World is Round*, published in 1939 and dedicated to a child of her acquaintance, comes close to much of Stein's other work in terms of the fluidity of expression and lack of rational structure, although there is a clear story-line. Recalling earlier children's texts, such as *At the Back of the North Wind* (see Chapter Four) and even *Mary Poppins*, which is discussed in detail in Chapter Eleven, the story's dependence on the ability of children to understand what might be beyond language attempts to say something about identity and reality in a playful rhyming way, while suggesting a sense of alienation.

> There at the school were other girls and Rose did not have quite as much time to sing and cry.
> The teachers taught her
> That the world was round
> That the sun was round
> That the moon was round
> That the stars were round
> And that they were all going around and around
> And not a sound.
> It was so sad it almost made her cry.
>
> (Stein 1993: 23–4)

Despite the sense of breaking away from conventional expression indicated by dependence of sound over sense, it is the suggestion of darkness beyond language that perhaps most forcibly characterises children's literature influenced by the Modernist aesthetic.

Although the majority of children's books attempted to reinforce notions of certainty and confidence and constructed safe worlds in which child characters could venture and return, the trend throughout the twentieth century was toward fiction which expressed the sense of alienation and anonymity more commonly expected in adult fiction.

The period between the wars, although productive, was strangely lacking in innovation or challenge. Harking back to earlier models of the school story and the adventure narrative, there is more produced which indicated the need to portray a safer world through fiction than to respond directly to events. However some writers, such as P.L. Travers and the 'Mary Poppins' stories (1934 onward) and John Masefield with *The Midnight Folk* (1927) and *Box of Delights* (1935), offered more innovative and sophisticated fantasies, as a response to modern experience. Otherwise, much of the fiction produced between the wars provided what Peter Hunt calls 'the characteristic voice of children's literature: clear, uncomplicated and generally neutral . . .' (1994: 120). For the most part, says Hunt, children's books of the 1920s and 1930s firmly established 'the tone of voice, the mode of telling, and the narrative contract between narrator and implied child reader' (1994: 106) that is familiar today. Critics also claim that the separate market for children in other media contributed to the kind of reading material being produced. Radio, animated films and children's periodicals all contributed the market value of fashioning material expressly for children. In America, too, the contained world of children's fiction was cushioned from the literary endeavours of F. Scott Fitzgerald, Ernest Hemingway and William Faulkner, among others. While these authors responded to social conflict at home and the effects of the war in Europe, many children's authors provided texts which reaffirmed earlier American values of hard work and positive thinking (Griswold 1992).

The work of Laura Ingalls Wilder, under the auspices of autobiographical fiction, rewrote the history of westward expansion. Her portraits of Pa Wilder in, for instance, *Little House on the Prairie* (1935), reflect the heroic qualities of the archetypal American hero of the frontier: building the family house from scratch, bravely facing wolves and dealing sympathetically with the Native American population. Although seemingly based on memory, Wilder's books are crafted carefully to meet the needs of the time and helped to reinforce national pride at the time of the New Deal. Economic hardship is seen, in her books, as an opportunity to exercise the virtues of self-sufficiency and family interdependency that were needed at that time.

Like Wilder, Arthur Ransome, with *Swallows and Amazons* (1930) and Enid Blyton in books too numerous to mention, provided their own versions of a 'real' world in which children could find an escape from the troubles of modernity. Achieving a sense of self-sufficiency without the assistance of adults (and often despite adult efforts), these narratives present an unquestioning portrayal of the time, protecting readers and offering them an unproblematised world.

The period immediately following the Second World War, however, brought a new complexity of tone to the form with a number of children's fantasy texts which, below the surface, delivered a darker message. The struggle to find identity, the uneasy relationship between the imagined and the real, and the changing perception of time are features of the aesthetic of late Modernism, which can be seen in many of the memorable children's texts of this period (Reynolds 1994). What is more, the narrative relationship embodied in many of these texts suggests a disruption of adult confidence in providing a sense of the world for children which at times approaches a postmodern sense of fracture and decentring.

The wealth of imaginative fiction for children in the 1950s has been discussed in many surveys of children's literature, in terms of the influence of world events on both the subject matter and tone in the American and British traditions. The aftermath of the Second World War and the threat of nuclear annihilation further enforce the expectation of apocalypse and thus make the possibilities of a better world more difficult to imagine. Because a way of looking with hope toward the future is often considered to be one of the key functions of children's books, the anxiety of the post-war period created challenges for children's authors. Now that children's publishing was firmly separated from the literary mainstream, authors were writing predominantly for child readers, rather than a mixed audience. While some authors, like C.S. Lewis, claimed to write for a non-specific audience (Lewis 1973), the simplicity of his narrative and perceived simplicity of vocabulary (Hunt 1991) limit the interest for adult readers.

What is most notable about a number of books of this period is the fact that there are many common elements within a range of texts. A shared sense that children must be offered something comforting, while acknowledging the darkness in a contemporary world, is communicated in books, such as Mary Norton's *The Borrowers* (1952), C.S. Lewis's *The Lion, the Witch and the Wardrobe* (1950) and other stories of Narnia, Philippa Pearce's *Tom's Midnight Garden* (1958) and Lucy Boston's *The Children of Green Knowe* (1954). All feature an old house in the country, and the presence of an older figure, who often performs the function of leading children into, or contributes to, elements of fantasy. The children in these books are isolated; either sent away from society because of illness (Norton, Pearce), wartime evacuation (Lewis) or convenience (Boston). The impression of exile seems to offer these children a chance to discover something redeeming which will help them in the difficult life ahead. The reality of loss pervades each book and it may be that these experiences signify the possibility of alternatives to 'real' experience. Recalling Mary Lennox's journey to Mistlethwaite Manor in *The Secret Garden*, the beginning of *The Children of Green Knowe* offers a description of Tolly travelling to Green Knowe. Images of the flooded landscape suggest The Flood and Tolly's arrival, a new beginning.

> A little boy was sitting in the corner of a railway carriage looking out at the rain, which was splashing downward in an ugly, dirty way. He was not the only person in the carriage, but the others were strangers to him. He was alone as usual . . . It was a stopping train – more stop than go – and it had been crawling along through flat flooded country for a long time. Everywhere there was water – not sea or rivers or lakes, but just senseless flood water with the rain splashing into it. Sometimes the railway lines were covered by it, and then the train-noise was quite different, softer than a boat.
>
> (Boston 1976: 3)

Similarly, in *The Magician's Nephew* (1952), Digory and Polly witness the birth of the new world of Narnia, and with it, a chance to discover, along with the other visitors to Narnia, an alternative reality.

These secondary worlds, or elements of fantasy intruding in the real world, often suggest uneasy truths. Tom, in *Tom's Midnight Garden* confronts the fact that he cannot live forever, even though he can share the Victorian past, and Wilbur, in *Charlotte's Web* (1952), by E.B. White, discovers, along with White's readers, the fact of death. *Charlotte's Web* is an extremely influential text and its relationship to Modernist thought and existentialism, in particular, is discussed more fully in Chapter Thirteen, but it is in the juxtaposition of fantasy with an actual, familiar world that it can be compared to the texts described above.

Although many of the children's books published since the war might be considered to depend on the experience of the 'real' child in a 'real' modern world, children's authors who combine the recognisable world with elements of the fantastic offer a more complex rendering of post-war angst – of a pessimistic view of 'civilisation' and an unease about the possibilities of speaking to children through fiction.

Narrative fractures and an underlying sense of doubt about the possible worlds offered in these fictions suggests a transitional phase as Modernism anticipates a postmodern response to an alienating and decentred world. It is in children's literature, which includes an implicit power relationship between adults and children in its reason for existence, that these fractures are most powerful. While a rejection or questioning of adult value systems is a feature of many of these texts and the unease of children in the modern world is a prominent subject, the sense of alienation is more clearly a feature of the narrative structure. Whether it is Tom's attempts to use the fracturing of time to allow him to live forever in the Midnight Garden or Wilbur's desperation to escape the butcher's knife in *Charlotte's Web*, children's fiction of the time is imbued with a sense of impending annihilation. While it is possible to attribute the apocalyptic mood of this post-war period to the memory of the Holocaust and the threat of atomic war, the search for individuality in an alienating social world is continually expressed in literature for both children and adults. The power of stories to construct reality is certainly played out in the self-conscious approach to writing for children.

The Borrowers by Mary Norton, discussed in more detail in Chapter Twelve, provides an example of the way these ideas are expressed in the children's fiction of the period. The isolation of both children, and the suggestion of their refugee status, raises doubts about what we all take for certainties: our identity and that of our place within a family/community/race.

The metafictional sense of the construction of a story like *The Borrowers* may have something in common with that self-aware archness that marked children's fiction of the *fin de siècle* period, yet it goes further than, for instance, E. Nesbit's playful sense of it. Here it is used to unsettle the reader's sense of confidence in the adult narrator; to pull away from the authorial role and relinquish the controlling power that fiction is typically seen to wield, particularly in texts for children.

In some ways, the implication of this new narrative relationship relies on the same notion of superior, childlike 'knowledge' derived from Romantic thought. The function of children's literature, to offer a comforting vision of the world, as well as to entertain, becomes more difficult as the social spheres of children and adults become more separate. At the same time, the creation of distinct children's publishing houses after the war reinforces that separation, suggesting an inevitable move away from the children's book with a dual audience, more familiar in the nineteenth century. Although many children's writers are writing for readers as a whole, the existence of a separate market often relegates these texts, no matter how valuable and relevant, to a tradition of lesser value.

The differentiation of the children's market to acknowledge the demands of a specifically adolescent readership signals the shift in perceptions of childhood, as well as a consciousness on the part of publishers capitalising on the perceived contrast of different readerships. Too 'adult' for children's stories, but not yet able to cope with 'adult' realities, teenage fiction from the 1960s challenged dominant social values and portrayed the break-up of the nuclear family. Though adolescent experience was also the subject of adult literature and film, the first-person address in J.D. Salinger's *Catcher in the Rye* (1951) expressed the spirit of rebellion and adolescent angst. The influence of this novel can be seen in the work of, for instance Paul Zindel, Robert Cormier and Aidan Chambers, all of whom break away from conventional narrative methods and approach a postmodern voice.

The chapters that follow offer readings of three children's books of the modern period that demonstrate the effects of the modernising trend in society on the Romantic notions of childhood and a childlike apprehension of the world. Each offers a different response to modernity and a different conception of its implied reader. *Mary Poppins* reveals similarities to writing for children of the nineteenth century, but hints at a Modernist aesthetic, while discussions of both *Charlotte's Web* and *The Borrowers* offer readings which identify the effect of late Modernism on books aimed at an exclusively young readership.

Chapter 11

Connecting with Mary Poppins

Pamela Lyndon Travers, the author of *Mary Poppins* (1934), was born in Australia in 1899 (Draper and Koralek 1999: 19). As a young woman she spent time in Ireland with W.B. Yeats, one of the great poets of the Modernist period, and was greatly influenced by him. Travers' work clearly fits closely within the Modernist frame of thinking. Apart from writing the *Poppins* books, P.L. Travers devoted a considerable amount of her life to studying Eastern philosophy and myths from across the world (Draper and Koralek 1990: 26) thus reflecting the Modernist break with Western forms of thinking, art and culture (Abrams 1999: 167).

Modernist writers sought new forms of literary expression which resisted the linear narratives and realism of the nineteenth century. Modernist writing is characterised by non-linear narratives, gaps in the text and a refusal to bring the work to closure and thus give absolute answers. The Modernist form of work is open and writerly, leaving the reader to make meaning through the text, rather than being directed by an omniscient narrator.

Travers identified her Modernist approach in a talk on the writing of *Mary Poppins* entitled 'Only Connect' (Egoff, Stubbs and Ashley 1969: 191–3). The title is taken from E.M. Forster's epigram to his Modernist novel, *Howard's End* (1910). What Travers identifies in Forster's work as attractive to her is also directly applicable to *Mary Poppins*, which can be read as an attempt to:

> link a passionate scepticism with the desire for meaning, to find the human key to the inhuman world about us; to connect the individual with the community, the known with the unknown; to relate the past to the present and both to the future.
>
> (Egoff, Stubbs and Ashley 1969: 184)

The emphasis in *Mary Poppins* is on the links which are made; the exhortation to '*only* connect' rather than achieve rationalised answers through connection. Travers took the reader from the certainties inherited from nineteenth-century realism, as for example in Francis Hodgson Burnett's *The Secret Garden* (1911), into the uncertainties of twentieth-century Modernism. Although Mary Lennox in Burnett's story begins her journey with much that is unknown, it is a journey of progressive discovery which leads to closure. Travers' text is a more diverse journey of experience, resisting such certainties and leading to an open ending. There are connections between the seemingly unrelated adventures besides the figure of Mary Poppins; however, the starting point for the experience of the reader and the community which surrounds the Banks' household is Mary herself.

The presence and nature of Mary Poppins is the central link in the text. The reader, the Banks household and the wider community gain experiences through Mary which suggest a philosophical approach to life, yet the philosophical approach itself is indirect and unstated. Travers' implied philosophical stance lies in the interaction between the 'real' world and the world of fantasy. Mary Poppins is the conduit between reality and fantasy, the structural interface in the text, so that there is no need for an intervening and obvious device, such as a wardrobe which leads into another world as in Lewis' *Narnia* stories which, although fantasy, are realist in their narrative form. Through Mary Poppins the real world dissolves into the world of the imagination where anything can happen at any time. Although Mary refuses to give explanations or to answer questions (like her creator P.L. Travers: see Egoff, Stubbs and Ashley 1969; Draper and Koralek 1999), the structure of the text enables readers to suggest their own conclusions because there is a pattern of connection which moves from the known to the unknown.

The direct address of the introduction gives the reader information in order to set them on a journey of exploration, with the inclusion of the reference to the Policeman giving an authority of reality: 'If you want to find Cherry Tree Lane all you have to do is ask the Policeman at the cross-roads' (Travers 1958: 11).

In the opening paragraphs, the only clue to the fantasy of other worlds is hinted at in the description of the cherry trees which go 'dancing right down the middle' (Travers 1958: 11) of the lane. The relationship between Mary Poppins and the landscape is central, activating the Romantic association between the self and nature, and thus forming a connection between Romanticism and Modernism. Travers' adherence to Romanticism is also linked with her creation of the other worlds, the other landscapes of the imagination, which are introduced through Mary Poppins.

In *Mary Poppins* Travers is also significantly concerned with the concept of the experience of childhood. The Banks household in Cherry Tree Lane is one which is focused upon children, rather than materiality. Mr and Mrs Banks have elected to have a large family rather than a prestigious house. The middle-class Banks family 'romantically' celebrates childhood, but it is out of joint without a nanny. The function of a nanny is to care for the children in the home and to link with the parents. Travers is implying that the demands and stresses of capitalism separate the middle-class Banks family from the enjoyment and wonder of childhood, despite their desires. Mr Banks, as his name suggests, works in a bank; he is, therefore, a servant of capitalist society. Mrs Banks, as a middle-class wife of the period, is caught between roles, for she is removed from the capacity to engage either in the workplace or effectively with her children. When Mary Poppins' predecessor leaves Mrs Banks spends her day 'writing letters to the papers and begging them to send some Nannies to her at once' (Travers 1958: 15), for in her role as their mother it is not within her to fully meet the needs of the children. The children themselves 'watched at the window and wondered who would come' (Travers 1958: 15).

Nature comes to the rescue of the Banks' household, symbolising a move toward a more 'natural' way of life. The East Wind transports Mary Poppins into Cherry Tree Lane, and in doing so, stimulates a level of movement in the cherry trees which amounts to physical animation, a different kind of life from the normally static rootedness of the trees. Blown by the wind, they looked as though they 'were dancing their roots out of the ground' (Travers 1958: 15). Against this background the children see Mary Poppins arrive as 'a shape', not a figure. 'Then the shape, tossed and bent under the wind, lifted the latch of the gate, and they could see that it belonged to a woman' (Travers 1958: 16).

The very nature of Mary Poppins is brought into question, for she is described as 'the shape' which 'belonged to a woman', not that the shape *was* a woman. From the outset Mary Poppins has a magical 'otherness' for the children which is connected with nature and the elements. Her physical appearance enhances this condition which is contained within a physical exteriority, for she is described by Jane as looking 'Rather like a Dutch wooden doll' (Travers 1958: 16). This intimates a conscious construction and an unreality. It also links Mary with the suggestion of toys and play. To the children she is at once a real figure of authority and didacticism as their nanny, and the fantastic facilitator of magical experiences. Furthermore Mary Poppins is a figure of actuality to the children in their known world, and a figure of mystery.

Mary Poppins' carpet bag symbolises the combination of actuality and mystery. It looks empty to Michael and Jane, nonetheless, Mary can withdraw items from it which are necessary for the well-being of the children and herself – 'a starched white apron', 'a large cake of Sunlight soap, a toothbrush, a packet of hairpins' and finally 'a large bottle labelled "One Tea-spoon to be Taken at Bed-Time"' (Travers 1958: 21). These are all objects she has placed there in her previous history: Mary's unknown past and their present are therefore interconnected. The carpet bag epitomises the function of Mary Poppins, which is to change the state of being for the better by drawing from her experiences, which nonetheless remain invisible to the children. The text works progressively from the immediate physical needs of the children to their imaginative and spiritual needs and well-being. Mary's medicine is pleasant and characteristically alters in relation to the particular patient, emphasising the individuality of interpretation available from a seemingly common experience. Three different colours and flavours are poured from the same medicine bottle: Michael's spoonful is 'dark crimson' and tastes of 'Strawberry ice'; Jane's is 'silvery, greeny, yellow' and the flavour of 'lime-juice cordial'; the twins' dose is suitably milk, whilst Mary Poppins very much enjoys her own 'Rum punch' (Travers 1958: 22–3). Travers' implied message here is that part of the process of growing up is to be able to realise one's individuality and accept differentiation. In these early stages the children are dependent upon Mary. Having taken his medicine, Michael is charmed by Mary and he is also anxious about whether she will leave, whilst Jane is seeking answers, demonstrating a desire for meaning in 'thinking about all that had happened, and wondering . . .' (Travers 1958: 24).

There will be much for the children and the reader to wonder about as their experiences with Mary Poppins and the text progress. Despite Travers' resistance to a linear narrative and this seeming lack of connection, the text is not a series of ad hoc events. There is a pattern which enables the reader to gain insight into the secret world of Poppins. The first pure fantasy adventure is when Mary goes off without the children on her day's holiday with Bert, the Match Man and pavement artist. It is, as it were, a day off from reality. Mary and Bert share an adult romantic relationship combined with the fantasy of magic as they move through the chalked frame of one of Bert's pavement pictures into a beautiful rural landscape where they are transformed into their best Sunday clothes, and take tea served by a waiter. (The waiter could not be seen in the actual chalk drawing because he was standing behind a tree.) Neither is much of the actual adventure of the day revealed, for all that is said by Travers is that they ride on the Merry-go-Round horses which take them 'all the way to Yarmouth and back'. In the first half of the twentieth century, Yarmouth was a popular seaside resort on the east coast where working class Londoners took their holidays. The fantasy world of Mary and Bert is a private one. On her return the children ask Mary where she has been; the response is 'Fairyland', to which the children reply 'It couldn't have been *our* Fairyland!' Mary Poppins' superior reply is 'Don't you know . . . that everybody's got a Fairyland of their own?' (Travers 1958: 38). Travers is emphasising the fact that the worlds of imagination are not constrained to childhood, neither are they necessarily open to everyone; one has to be invited in and the fantasy shared. The progression of the text continues to elucidate this position as Travers leads the children and the reader on a safe journey into other worlds and ways of thinking which they share with Mary Poppins and her people.

Travers expands the world of fantasy by incorporating different communities. The degree of suspension of belief required to accept the fantasy is controlled in the text by working progressively outward from the immediate relationship between the nanny and her charges. In these early stages of learning about fantasy worlds the experience is based on activities engaged in by the children, and then in the activities of the immediate community. The children are taken to meet Mary's relations and experience physical liberation through pleasure in the uncontrollable and liberating laughter shared with her uncle – an experience of laughing so much that it elevates them to the ceiling. They meet her friends in the fantastic confectioners, where the actual fingers of sweet-makers become candy. The fantasy world then moves a little more widely into the actuality of the Banks' neighbourhood and an adventure privy only to Mary. She helps Andrew, the pampered, yet frustrated pedigree dog of Miss Lark, to find a canine friend. Miss Lark is a grand and snobbish lady who cannot understand Andrew's friendship with an undesirable mongrel. The episode demonstrates Mary Poppins' power to understand and communicate with the animals, and also Travers belief in the power of friendship which crosses the false boundaries of class.

Having established a link between real activity and fantasy, Travers moves one stage further and introduces a fantasy created entirely through narrative. When Jane is unwell, Mary Poppins tells her the story of the dancing Red Cow and the star. The story is logically well-placed, in that a sick child would retreat into another's adventure rather than have the energy to expend on their own. Jane sees the cow through the window, wandering down Cherry Tree Lane. From this simple starting point Mary weaves a story of a cow who could not stop dancing because she had a star caught on her horn. The only way she can free herself is to jump over the moon, linking the old nursery rhyme with Mary Poppins' own created world which she shares with the sick child. In contrast the following episode of Michael's 'Bad Tuesday' is about an excess of negative energy expressed in Michael's naughtiness. His all-encompassing adventure takes him around the world, guided by Mary Poppins' own compass. He meets children from the four corners of the earth, burning up his excess energy in a positive manner. The end of his disturbing day is not in fantasy but in the real security and love extended by Mary Poppins, despite his behaviour, as she brings him a warm cup of milk at bedtime, and tucks him cosily into bed. Travers understands that children cannot always be good and controlled and that they need to express their emotions within a secure framework of love and tolerance.

These and subsequent fantasy sequences build into a pattern of interconnection. Elements recur through the adventures, such as Mary's people – Bert and the confectioners, for example – and members of the local community, Miss Lark and the Admiral. Animals met earlier also return. There is also a particular focus on the stars which plays a recurrently important part in symbolising a union between the known world and the ethereal. The Red Cow has to leap over the moon; Mary Poppins, Miss Fanny, Miss Annie and Mrs Corry, the confectioners, glue gingerbread stars into the night sky to give a golden light; whilst the final adventure before Mary leaves is when the children meet Maia, one of the Pleiades who has come down from the heavens to buy Christmas presents for her sisters, Electra and Merope.

Travers further emphasises her notion of unity through fantasy by including the episodes with the babies John and Barbara, which demonstrates the beginnings of the disruption of interconnection in the early stages of childhood. John and Barbara lie in their cots in the nursery, which is the centre of Mary Poppins' domain. They are in harmony with their surroundings in the fullest Romantic sense, as they talk to the sunlight and the starling, but the demands of the cycles of nature itself disrupt this idyllic unity. The sun has to travel from East to West in a day; the starling has matters to attend to; whilst the babies will mature, learn to speak, and their teeth will come through. Gaining their teeth will take them into the food chain as predatory consumers in the real world. They will no longer be able to communicate from the security of harmony which melds together the worlds of the real and the fantastic. Travers identifies language as the site where her dream of inter-connectedness is fractured as the babies move from the prelinguistic state into articulate beings: in Lacanian terms, from the imaginary into the symbolic order of language. Paradoxically, language is Travers' means of unlocking the doors into other worlds, her 'human key' to the 'inhuman world about us'.

Travers highlights the inhuman nature of humanity in the climactic nocturnal visit to the Zoo on Mary's birthday. The process of enabling the reader to make connections has been leading to this sur-real focal episode which is Mary's special day. The intensity of the forces of nature is magnified. The children have an extreme desire to follow Mary, which is embodied in an unseen voice urging them on. The power of Travers'/Poppins' alternative world of imagination culminates in a carnivalesque, and politically charged, scene where the animals are liberated and the people caged. The Admiral and politicians, for example, when caged are exposed as the rather unpleasant human beings they really are. It is the freed animals who are noble and gracious. Travers is implying that it is impossible to understand the world from a humanist perspective of tolerance and interrelationship if we are trapped within the cage of materialist reality and cruelty. She is also suggesting, through drawing on Eastern philosophy and mythology in this episode – as opposed to Western – that the hierarchical power structures of Western culture and philosophy are inadequate and destructive. Mary's birthday party epitomises tolerance and connection as the animals join together in the Great

Chain which forms a circle. The enmity of predator and victim is set aside as 'the small are free from the great and the great protect the small' (Travers 1958: 184). The King of the Animal world, the snake, the Hamadryad, summarises this notion of interconnected unity as all there gathered rock in a unified harmony.

> 'Bird and beast and stone and star – we are all one, all one –' murmured the Hamadryad . . .
>   'Child and serpent, star and stone – all one.'
> (Travers 1958: 187).

The children are rocked into a sleep from which they awake finding they that they have shared the same dream. As individuals, Jane and Michael have enjoyed communal connection; they have linked the known with the unknown. They will carry their past dreams into the future, with thanks to their nanny. The function of Mary Poppins has been as an educator, a means of connection with other worlds, whilst refusing to give final answers and closure. Her refusal to give answers has meant that the children have had to live with uncertainty, and through her learn trust and the ability to construct their own continuing or elaborating narrative. Their time with Mary has inculcated and reinforced a positive attitude in the unknown, for each adventure has been enjoyable and educative. They have learnt that there is security in *not* knowing if one has the right philosophical, i.e. Modernist, frame of mind, which can contemplate the most fundamental reality of life, which is loss. The pain of such loss, the loss of the innocent Romantic longing for childhood and worlds of fantasy is a painful awareness in Modernist thinking. However, what Travers does is to give her children/readers the strength and power of hope, for they can create and recreate adventures with Mary Poppins in their own fantastic and individual worlds. Mary Poppins has to leave them physically – as we all must depart finally through death – but spiritually she lives in their dreams, and their fantasies. She will therefore return in the 'reality' of the imagination whenever they want to remake and/or extend the story of the time spent with Mary, by 'only connecting'.

Chapter 12

Spinning the word
Charlotte's Web

The American author, Elwyn Brooks White (1899–1985) wrote his Modernist text, *Charlotte's Web* in 1952, during the post-war period when there was an overarching mood of uncertainty derived from the aftermath of the Second World War. In *Charlotte's Web*, White explores the individual's relationship to the great uncertainties of life and death, friendship and love, whilst also providing an unsentimentalised sense of comfort in a dark world. This is achieved through the relationships between the genres of realism and fantasy employed in the text, and also White's interplay between Romanticism, Modernism and Existentialism.

Charlotte's Web draws on Romanticism in the focus on the importance of childhood, the notion of innocence, and the powerful use of landscape and setting. The influence of Modernism is clearly to be seen in the fractured notion of this text, as White shifts between realism and fantasy, and clearly critiques the materialist value system of the adult world. The philosophical position of existentialism *per se*, places emphasis on the uniqueness and isolation of the individual experience in a world which is seen as hostile or indifferent. Human existence is inexplicable to the existentialists, and stresses freedom of choice and the individual taking responsibility for the consequences of their own acts. White's Modernist sensibility and orientation towards existentialism enable him to engage the reader with a sense of uncertainty, and to explore the inexplicable and ever present tensions between life and death.

White expressed his 'innate' orientation towards existentialism as follows:

> Intuitively, I've always been aware of the vitally important pact which a man has with himself, to be all things to himself, and

to be identified with all things, to stand self-reliant, taking advantage of this haphazard connection with a planet, riding his luck, and following his bent with the tenacity of a hound.

(Griffiths 1980: 111)

Charlotte's Web is set on a farm in Massachusetts where eight-year-old Fern lives with her parents and her brother Avery. The realistic opening scene of the book stresses Fern's movement towards responsibility as she takes a stand against her father to rescue Wilbur, a piglet, who is to be slaughtered because he is the runt of the litter. Fern undertakes the job of raising the piglet. Wilbur's situation in the text is as a functional farm animal whose fate balances between life and death, subject to the decisions of others. Fern's experience in the narrative is the movement from childhood to preparation for adult responsibility. Both Fern and Wilbur are travelling from innocence to experience in their different ways. A good deal of this journey is depicted through the love of caring which grows in Fern as she nurtures the piglet, and the dependency and love which grows in Wilbur, as he is raised by Fern. Wilbur has a second 'nurturer' who is Charlotte, a spider. Charlotte is Wilbur's friend, guide, and saviour. Her wisdom is made available through the textual device of fantasy, in that the animals can talk to each other, although not to humans. Charlotte is able to talk to Wilbur and to weave words into her web which bring about 'magical' transformations in the decisions and actions of the humans who can read the spun messages in her web. E.B. White thus spins realism and fantasy together to create *Charlotte's Web*.

There is a Modernist consciousness throughout White's text in the sense of uncertainty to which Wilbur is subjected in the precariousness of his fate as a farm animal being bred for meat production. The emphasis on the self in *Charlotte's Web* is also central to Modernism, as is the implied sense of being alone. The tone of self-reliance and determination demonstrated both by Fern and by Charlotte, and to a certain extent by the rat Templeton, albeit in a less attractive manner, reflects the pioneering spirit of America. White's overall alignment with the real rather than the sentimental is also of the American tradition. (See Avery [1994] for a full discussion of the relationship between realism and the sentimental in American children's literature.) However, White employs fantasy as a narrative strategy to engage with the philosophical and moral realities which lie at the heart of his text. E.B. White does not shy away from the reality that death is part of the experience of the living, nor that we die alone. The recurrent threats to Wilbur's life and the lonely death of Charlotte attest to this. White uses the oppositions of life and death to explore his moral position, which is that morality is the responsibility of the individual. Furthermore, the moral position is judged by the reader on the actions of the characters. It is the reader who makes meaning throughout this Modernist text, rather than an omniscient narrator.

The narrative structure of *Charlotte's Web* enables the reader to negotiate White's philosophical and moral contexts. His construction of character, the physical settings, the shifts between reality and fantasy, and his particular use of language work together within an integral relationship. There is no clear division into those characters who are 'good', or those who are 'evil'. Each character has a set of characteristics which pertain to tendencies, yet it is their actions in any one particular circumstance which carry moral weight. The central characters are Fern, Wilbur and Charlotte. Fern is determined, caring and able to take responsibility. At the beginning of the story she argues her case strongly to save the then unnamed piglet from slaughter, saying that just because he is weak he should not be killed as a matter of course. She equates the piglet with her position as a child, appealing to her parents' sense of humanity. From the point that she assumes responsibility for the animal, and takes on a mothering role, the piglet begins to develop an identity in the mind of the reader. It is language – that is, the naming of Wilbur – which marks his transition from a farm animal to one having an identity and character. Initially Fern treats Wilbur like a human baby; however, White refuses to allow Wilbur to evolve sentimentally as a replacement child. In realist terms Wilbur must take his place as a farm animal, and is moved to the Zuckerman farm to be raised as a pig, who, the reader predicts, is destined to end up as the Christmas roast.

The use of setting plays a functional role in. the narrative structure of the text, echoing the Romantic association between the self and place. One community of human characters is associated with Fern in the domestic scenes, and the running of the farm, whilst a second community of animal characters are associated with Wilbur in the barn. There are parallels between both sets of characters, who act as choruses to the central action between Fern and Wilbur. The humans and the animals are both supportive of Fern and Wilbur, however, there is no false sentimentality for it is clear to all parties that farm animals are bred for food production. Herein lies the ever-present threat to Wilbur and, one of the central uncertainties of the text for the reader and for Wilbur.

There are also further pressures on the well-being of both Fern and Wilbur, in that there are two potentially threatening and seemingly untrustworthy characters: Fern's brother, Avery, and the rat, Templeton, who lives in the barn. Both Avery and Templeton are self-centred, somewhat jealous and attention-seeking. Avery is also inclined to be violent. He carries a gun, is overactive, and at one point endangers Charlotte. Although their characters are equally problematic, as the plot works out, they both act in socially positive ways, despite their natural inclinations. For example, after some persuasion Templeton finds magazine clippings for Charlotte to help her select words to weave into her web to save Wilbur. Avery unexpectedly becomes the comic centre of attention in the fairground at the moment of Wilbur's triumph, when Fern is absent. His uncontrolled energy is diverted into clowning, which, to some extent, softens the sadness of the fact that Fern is disappointingly absent. She is more interested in her emergent romantic associations with a young fellow, instead of being there to celebrate Wilbur's triumph, as the reader would hope, and expect in a sentimentalised text. E.B. White's position here is again that of the Modernist writer. Throughout the text White presents a Modernist understanding of subjectivity, which considers the self in relation to the circumstances, rather than reacting in a fixed manner with unchangeable predetermined character traits. Fern is not the reliable classic heroine, ever at Wilbur's side. Neither are Avery and Templeton classic heroes, for there is no fundamental change of character displayed.

The 'heroic' focus of the text is divided between Fern and Charlotte, who are moral heroines. They both act in unselfish and self-determined ways to save Wilbur through their words and their actions. Fern saves him verbally through her initial argument with her parents, and then by nurturing and befriending him. The inter-relationship between language and action recurs throughout the text, for Charlotte is initially introduced as a disembodied friendly voice in the barn, when Wilbur is lonely and despairing. White's presentation of Charlotte as a spider is technically accurate and unsentimentalised. He describes the intelligence and capabilities of arachnids. Charlotte, the spider, is functionally a highly effective hunter and killer. Charlotte, the character, is maternal, loving and generous. The oppositions in Charlotte's personality are irreconcilable from a humanist perspective; in the real world of survival where nature is red in tooth and claw, they are understandable. There again is White's Modernist resistance to inflexible categorisation, for the exact nature of the self is always intangible. White realises Charlotte's intellectual capability as linguistic aptitude. It is only through language that we can know of the 'real' Charlotte. Ironically, it is the fantastic device of making insects and animals speak, and transferring human traits to the animal and insect world, which enables White to explore this position. He thus employs fantasy to explore the relationship between the self and nature. The central physical site of exploration is the Zuckermans' barn where Wilbur spends his 'adolescent' life after being weaned by Fern.

In *Charlotte's Web*, White's use of setting, like characterisation, changes in relation to circumstance. It is the perception of the circumstances which determines the character's emotional reaction to the physicality of place. Wilbur is initially idyllically happy in the barn. He has everything a pig could physically need, plus the love and attention of Fern. When Fern is unable to visit him Wilbur becomes lonely and bored; the barn is then perceived by him as restrictive and uninteresting. Wilbur is encouraged by the Goose to make a bid for freedom; he makes an unsuccessful escape. Interestingly he cannot see the Goose, only hear her: again language is the primary source of influence. In his moments of freedom, Wilbur luxuriates in typical pig behaviour, rooting up a patch of ground in the orchard (White 1963: 23); however, he does not actually know what to do with his freedom beyond those immediate acts, for he has had no experience of being outside alone, and has no function outside of the farmyard. Wilbur is a relieved and happy pig when he readily succumbs to being coaxed back into the barn with food. White reflects on Wilbur's subjective relationship to the world '"I'm really too young to go out into the world alone," he thought . . .' (White 1953: 28).

Ultimately even Wilbur, who is innocently receptive to his circumstances, cannot endure loneliness. Although all his physical needs are amply met as he is being well-fed and fattened up in the barn, spiritually he is bereft. He is lonely, lacks a sense of purpose and becomes depressed. Even just eating is not enough for a pig. '"I'm less than two months old and I'm tired of living"' (White 1963: 20).

As John Griffiths elaborates:

> White thus establishes Wilbur in a desperate existential situation: he is scared of dying: he faces *ennui*, and is starved for friendship and love. These are the psychic problems attendant on the 'haunting intimation' that one is ultimately alone.
>
> (Griffiths 1980: 113)

This is also a reflection of a Modernist standpoint on modern life.

Wilbur falls into a depressive state, from which he is rescued by Charlotte's friendship. Her friendly, encouraging, and, initially, anonymous voice in the darkness gives him a reason to look forward to daybreak. He now has a purpose for living. At this point Wilbur becomes distraught when he learns that he is to be butchered for the Christmas feast. For him the barn has become a place of entrapment, whereas once it was a haven, a piggy heaven.

Wilbur's salvation is, once again, through language and friendship; this time principally from Charlotte. From this point on Fern becomes a passive observer, learning about an other world of nature. As E.B. White pointed out in an interview: 'Fern is a listener, and a translator' (Wintle and Fisher 1974: 131). If she had been able to talk with the animals in the style of Doctor Dolittle, the philosophical focus of the work would have shifted from realism to fantasy. Fern is a silent mediator who cannot break the boundaries between the human and the animal worlds. When Fern tries to bridge the two worlds and tell her mother of the events in the barn her mother thinks she is ill and takes her to the doctor. Doctor Dorian takes an understanding and sympathetic stance, as does her father, both saying, in their different ways, that 'Children pay better attention than grown-ups' (White 1963: 107).

There is the recognition by White that these two linguistic worlds cannot intermingle in the normal sense. However Charlotte, the spider, is magically able to join the two worlds through her written communication.

Charlotte is rational, creative and a realist who applies her intelligence in an imaginative way. Through Charlotte, the intelligence of the insect world is translated into language. By 'miraculously' spinning she uses a web of language to entrap the gullible humans. They become the 'victims' of her ploy. Wilbur is changed from a victim into a hero, when Charlotte spins the words 'Some pig' into her web to focus the humans' positive attention on Wilbur. Wilbur becomes the subject of Charlotte's spun words.

> 'Well', said Mrs Zuckerman, 'it seems to me you're a little off. It seems to me that we have no ordinary *spider.*'
> 'Oh, no,' said Zuckerman, 'It's the pig that's unusual. It says so, right there in the middle of the web.'
>
> (White 1963: 81)

Language is at the centre of Charlotte's web. Her web is a creation which highlights an area of space rather than a solid construction which occupies space. It is a network which produces a framework so that the invisible becomes visible: language becomes a substance. Through the device of fantasy, White has, transitorily, solved the central problem of Modernism which is how to fix language as a substantive entity. He has also produced a set of circumstances which illustrate the slippage of meaning which surrounds language. Without performing any action himself, Wilbur has moved from being an innocent and passive subject, about to be slaughtered to fulfil his life function as a farm animal, to an icon of wonder, a subject to be preserved. Wilbur has passively moved from victim to hero by the force of language. It is Charlotte's words which have made the difference in how the humans perceive Wilbur. The implication here is that meaning is unfixed. Wilbur as signifier has remained unchanged; what is signified is different. The position clearly portrayed to the reader is that the truth lies in the 'real' effect of Charlotte's language, for her physical effort to save Wilbur is described by White as 'a trick' (White 1963: 84). White also satirises the local community, portraying the people as susceptible and gullible, for they think that this is a wondrous and miraculous sign, for which they give thanks in church. Wilbur is changed in their perception, and so the barn also changes for Fern. Once a place of peaceful communion with nature, it is now the centre of attention for the local people, who clamour to see the miraculous pig.

Life is changing for all the characters. Wilbur is the centre of attention. Fern is moving away from her mothering role as others take part in the preparation of Wilbur for the competition at the fair. Charlotte herself is preparing for motherhood as she moves through her functional reproductive cycle. Wilbur can easily (and enthusiastically!) change into the physical image of a prized pig, simply by fulfilling his animal functions and eating. Fern has also to grow into another stage of life, as she changes from a child into an adolescent. The fairground is the scene of change – symbolically they move on the Ferris wheel of life. The fairground is the place of judgement for Wilbur and for Fern. Wilbur is to be judged in the competition: Fern is to be judged by the reader, as she chooses to ride into adolescence on the Ferris wheel with her new young love rather than stay with Wilbur, her childhood passion. The expectation of the reader in a closed text would be that Fern would be there to support Wilbur to the end. In this open-ended, Modernist text, Fern follows her own interests, as she prefers to ride the Ferris wheel with her new boyfriend rather than stay with a pig.

The final conversation between Charlotte and Wilbur affirms White's philosophical and moral position:

> 'You have been my friend,' replied Charlotte. 'That in itself is a tremendous thing. I wove my webs for you because I liked you. After all, what's life, anyway? We're born, we live a little while, we die. A spider's life can't help being something of a mess, with all this trapping and eating flies. By helping you, perhaps I was trying to lift up my life a trifle. Heaven knows anyone's life can stand a little of that.'
>
> (White 1963: 157)

The reality is that the Ferris wheel of life turns on. White encapsulates the Romantic longing for the enduring idealised relationship of total fulfilment, with the poignant realisation that the ideal can never be achieved, that there must always be movement, change and loss. Charlotte has fulfilled her function, she has produced her young and died a lonely death. Fern is journeying onward into her future with her new male friend, her innocent childhood is moving into the past. Wilbur, nonetheless, has been saved by friendship and love, a salvation which encloses the reader in the realities of life, whilst also giving a hope of continuity and security in an uncertain and changing world. Wilbur continues his life in the barn with Charlotte's offspring. Charlotte is, in a way, dead but undying; she is held in the web of memory, the language of the mind. E.B. White leaves the reader with the realities of life and death, and the security drawn from the hope of love and friendship.

Chapter 13

Real or story?

The Borrowers

The lack of a central reality implied by a response to the experience of the modern world typifies many of the enduring children's texts of the 1950s. Mary Norton, in *The Borrowers*, pushes the boundaries farther and suggests, through many layers of meaning, the difficulties of offering children stories about the world in the post-war age.

First published in 1952, this story of the little people living under the floorboards remains a popular text today, enjoying numerous adaptations for television and film. The fascination with the miniature family led to four sequels, though it is the richness and complexity of the narrative of the first story that reflects most strongly a Modernist sensibility and response to the sense of alienation in the mid-twentieth century.

In common with several other memorable children's texts of the decade, *The Borrowers* provides the juxtaposition of an identifiable 'real' world with an element of the fantastic. As the works of Lucy Boston, C.S. Lewis and E.B. White also demonstrate, the blurring of boundaries between the real and the fantastic can provide both a sense of escape and of unease. The detail of the translation of familiar 'lost' objects into miniature household goods provides an imaginary world of play, similar to playing with a living doll's house. While the reader is at once encouraged to identify with the boy's encounters with the Clocks as 'make-believe', the philosophy of 'making-do' allows the book to be read as a metaphor for rationing during the Second World War. And though the search for other Borrowers can be viewed in terms of its place in the tradition of an adventure/quest story, it is also a reflection of the situation of the refugee or the stateless family arising out of the end of the war. The possibility that the Clocks are the only family of Borrowers remaining is an allusion to the experience, not only of the evacuee, as suggested by Kimberley Reynolds (1994), but of the Jews hiding out, or threatened with extermination by gas. Even the choice of the stopped clock as a reference point for the Borrowing family signals a disruption of time and the threat of disorder familiar to readers of much post-war literature.

If the fact of the Second World War and the growing alienation of individual experience in the modern world can be seen to inflect the stories one is able to tell children, then *The Borrowers* demonstrates this influence on a number of different levels. Reynolds emphasises the changing structure of the family and, in particular, shifting gender roles in her reading of Norton's work, and other critics call attention to Norton's portrayal of class-consciousness in Homily's 'upward-mobility' and the double-barrelled names of many of the Borrowing families. However, it is the element of foreboding in the encounters between Arrietty Clock and the boy which embodies the sensibility of late Modernism.

By using the conventional trope of the child separated from his parents: the boy has been sent back to England from India to convalesce from rheumatic fever – Norton relies on the readers' expectations of such texts as Burnett's *The Secret Garden,* only to overturn them. Whereas Mary's aberrant behaviour is normalised in her exposure to nature and the archetypal Romantic figure of Dickon, neither the boy nor Arrietty can offer the other a way of resolving their displacement.

Norton shifts the focalising narrative between the two to prevent one viewpoint from dominating, and uses continual reference to light and shadow to dramatise the fear of alienation in both children. The garden in which the boy and Arrietty meet is no longer a redeeming place but a threatening space, where identity is questioned and isolation is emphasised.

> Arrietty burst out laughing; she laughed so much that she had to hide her face in the primrose. 'Oh dear,' she gasped with tears in her eyes, 'you are funny!' She stared upwards at his puzzled face. 'Human beans are *for* Borrowers – like bread's for butter!'
>
> The boy was silent a while. A sigh of wind rustled the cherry-tree and shivered among the blossom.
>
> 'Well, I don't believe it,' he said at last, watching the falling petals. 'I don't believe that's what we're for at all and I don't believe we're dying out!'

'Oh, goodness!' exclaimed Arrietty impatiently, staring up at his chin. 'Just use your common sense: you're the only real human bean I ever saw (although I do just know of three more – Crampfurl, Her, and Mrs Driver). But I know lots and lots of Borrowers: the Overmantels and the Harpsichords and the Rain-Barrels and the Linen-Presses and Boot-Racks and the Hon. John Studdingtons and –'

He looked down. 'John Studdington? But he was our grand-uncle –'

'Well, this family lived behind a picture,' went on Arrietty, hardly listening, 'and there were the Stove-Pipes and the Bell-Pulls and the –'

'Yes,' he interrupted, 'but did you see them?'

'I saw the Harpsichords. And my mother was a Bell-Pull. The others were before I was born . . .'

He leaned closer. 'Then where are they now? Tell me that.'

'My Uncle Hendreary has a house in the country,' said Arrietty coldly. Edging away from his great lowering face; it was misted over, she noticed, with hairs of palest gold. 'And five children, Harpsichords and Clocks.'

'But where are the others?'

'Oh,' said Arrietty, 'they're somewhere.' But where? she wondered. And she shivered slightly in the boy's cold shadow which lay about her, slant-wise, on the grass.

(Norton 1995: 73)

The falling petals, the shivering of the wind, and the shadow of the boy threaten each child's sense of certainty and identity. Although the reader can easily rely on the reality of the human boy and the truth of the isolation and dissolution of the Borrowers as a race, Norton's method invites the possibility of uncertainty to invade the narrative. The confusion over the painting of John Studdington raises further questions over how one 'proves' one's existence: the boy's uncle may be just as distant to him as the Hon. John Studdingtons are to Arrietty. By leaving the question unresolved, Norton suggests an equally tenuous connection between the portrait as evidence of each race, and of each child's identification with that race.

The threat of the post-war world to a coherent sense of individual identity is articulated here as a result of isolation and the separation of children and adults. As Arrietty attempts both to challenge the conventional gender roles and to venture outside of her parents' circle of influence, so the boy contravenes human rules of property to become a 'Borrower'. His sense of belonging, in this way, to Arrietty's family is a replacement for his own absent family and the cold emptiness of Great Aunt Sophy's home. This rejection of his identification with the human family is forcefully dramatised by the episode in which he attacks the fabric of the house in order to set the Clocks free. The violence of his efforts restarts the hall clock and seems to suggest that his 'time' begins with this act of freedom and defiance.

However, even this sense of resolution is undercut by Norton's framing narrative. We know from the beginning of the story that the boy will die a 'hero's death' on the Northwest Frontier, casting an ironic shadow over his heroic actions on behalf of the Borrowers.

It is the sense of doubt at the heart of Norton's narrative, however, which places the text so firmly within a late Modernist aesthetic. At times, in fact, Norton suggests a postmodern playfulness in her tendency to prevent the reader from arriving at a position of certainty. On one level, we are continually teased, as Mrs May teases Kate, about the trustworthiness of the boy as a storyteller and, thus, about the existence of the Borrowers. On a deeper level, though, the confusion of narrative frames calls attention to the storytelling act in such a way that the book as a whole expresses a sense of uncertainty about the very act of telling. While Norton uses the adult storyteller, Mrs May, with her child audience, Kate, as a frame, she casts doubt on the relationship from the opening paragraph:

> It was Mrs May who first told me about them. No, not me. How could it have been me – a wild, untidy, self-willed little girl who stared with angry eyes and was said to crunch her teeth? Kate, she should have been called. Yes, that was it – Kate. Not that the name matters much either way: she barely comes into the story.
>
> (Norton 1995: 1)

The sudden shift from first person to third person signals a lack of confidence in the narrative that further distances the reader from the possibility of a trustworthy relationship between teller and told. What is more striking, however, is the denial of identity implied by the rejection of the original first-person narrator to tell the story.

The question 'how could it have been me' at once casts doubt on the 'truth' of the storytelling event, but also suggests doubt in the narrator's mind about her own childhood past. Throughout the story, shifts in point of view from chapter to chapter and parenthetical remarks that anticipate future events, interrupt and disturb the flow of a single storytelling voice that one might be led to expect. At other times, Norton calls attention to the constructedness of the story and further undermines the reader's ability to rely on the narrative.

'But I do remember,' said Mrs May. 'Oddly enough I remember it better than many real things which have happened. Perhaps it was a real thing. I just don't know.'

(Norton 1995: 6)

The ending, too, provides a culmination of Norton's many narrative intrusions, creating a metafictive layer of meaning. When Mrs May announces the end, Norton subverts and resubverts the reader's expectations of the ending of a children's story, playfully defamiliarising the adult/child relationship at the heart of the activity.

'And that,' said Mrs May, laying down her crochet hook, 'is really the end.'

Kate stared at her. 'Oh, it can't be,' she gasped, 'oh, please ... please ...'

'The last square,' said Mrs May, smoothing it out on her knee, 'the hundred and fiftieth. Now we can sew them together –'

'Oh,' said Kate, breathing again, 'the quilt! I thought you meant the story.'

'It's the end of the story too,' said Mrs May absently, 'in a way,' and she began to sort out the squares.

'But,' stammered Kate, 'you can't – I mean –' and she looked, quite suddenly, everything they had said she was – wild, self-willed, and all the rest of it. 'It's not fair,' she cried, 'it's cheating. It's –' Tears sprang to her eyes; she threw her work down on the table and darning needle after it, and she kicked the bag of wools which lay beside her on the carpet.

'But something more did happen,' said Mrs May, 'a lot more happened. I'm going to tell you.'

'Then why did you say it was the end?'

'Because,' said Mrs May (she still looked surprised), 'he never saw them again.'

'Then how can there be more?'

'Because,' said Mrs May, 'there is more.'

Kate glared at her. 'All right,' she said, 'go on.'

Mrs May looked back at her. 'Kate,' she said after a moment, 'stories never really end. They can go on and on and on. It's just that sometimes, at a certain point, one stops telling them.'

(Norton 1995: 138–9)

While this passage does many things: recalling the tension between Kate's narrative stance of the opening passage, echoing the boy's radical behaviour at the close of his story in Kate's kicking of the wool and, at the same time, her resistance to Mrs May's authority over the story, Norton's playfulness teasingly undermines the expectation of closure.

Her way of telling suggests that stories for children are not merely 'told'; they are as much a part of the teller's attempt to sort the real from the imaginary. In this way, *The Borrowers* is a text that breaks away from the sense of adult confidence and power to provide a fictional world. The narrator can know no more than the reader can; 'reality' is no more than a never-ending story.

Section V

Postmodernism

Chapter 14

Playful subversion

There are many contested definitions of postmodernism, and the difficulties of locating the relationship between Modernism and postmodernism suggest a complexity that might be expected to exclude children's literature. However, it is precisely the nature of the task of writing for children, and the power relations entailed in that act, which forge a special link between children's literature and postmodernist responses to cultural change. By including children's literature in a map of literary history it is possible to see the postmodern tendency in art and literature as a return to or, perhaps, a reinterpretation of the radicalism of a Romantic view of the adult/reader relationship.

Postmodern theorists, such as Lyotard, challenge the credibility of the master narratives that have dominated cultural production since the Enlightenment (Brooker 1992). Although this position may appear to dismiss the essentialism of Romantic constructions of childhood, the implied reader of postmodern children's literature is still defined in Romantic terms. The techniques that define the texts discussed in this chapter as postmodern, as well as those discussed in the chapters that follow, may be subversive and liberating, yet the public 'use' of children's literature continues to marginalise its experimental and aesthetic value.

The marginalisation of writing for children and its link with popular culture place it in a relationship with definitions of high culture that are constantly contested in postmodern formulations. In addition, the inequity of the relationship between the 'adult, knowing' author and the 'innocent, receptive' child, and the uneasy assumption that stories can be repositories of universal truths, are all involved in the discourses which surround art, culture and politics in this postmodern epoch. In contrast to the growing market in branded children's books and series fiction, which echoes trends in pulp publishing for adults, the invitations to engage in subversive playfulness and the deconstructive tendencies of some children's books demand a comparison with the most radical postmodern challenges in art.

Challenges to the credibility of the metanarratives of Enlightenment absolutes suggest an impossible relationship between the Romantic images of childhood as essentially innocent, and the postmodern strategies that characterise the most exciting contemporary children's literature.

While the rejection of absolutes and essentialist thinking defines the ideolog(ies) of postmodernism, if something so shapeshifting can be said to offer ideologies, the techniques that mark individual texts for children provide a more open reading experience that often appears to rely on an idea of children reminiscent of the Romantic notions of the pre-social infant. The elements of subversion present, particularly, in contemporary picturebooks, for example, invite children as readers to form a powerful relationship to the text and reinforce the relationship between postmodernism and romantic anarchism suggested by Brooker (1992). Parodic gestures, narrative fractures and metafictional strategies which call attention to the improving qualities of literature can all be found in recent work for children, such as the work of John Scieszka and Lane Smith discussed in Chapter Sixteen. Such features act as a challenge to dominant constructions of childhood and refer to an implied reader reminiscent of that posited by George MacDonald (see Chapter Four).

The web of discourses which surround children and their reading activities: journalists, educationalists, parents, etc., articulate an overwhelming anxiety about the effects of contemporary society on notions of childhood as, in some way, ideal. The fracture of human relations, most often seen in the shifts in family structures, and the power of technology and media, appear to threaten admittedly Romantic conceptions of innocence (Reynolds 1994). The child, removed from the 'norms' of the nuclear family and the certainties of organised religion, consumed by materialism and the proliferation of sexualised, 'adulterated' images of the body, has become a threatening, uncontrollable force. Children can be murderers and, as such, signify a society which is out of control.

While more and more children's books, such as Melvin Burgess' *Junk* (1998) and Robert Swindell's *Stone Cold* (1994) reflect these concerns, they are often attacked for their hard realism, further demonstrating contemporary fears that children as readers will become the damaged youths they read about. The moralising discourse that assumes a direct relationship between the reading of fiction and aberrant behaviour rejects the attempt, on the part of authors, to invite (and expect) children to think for themselves. This reactionary attitude is reminiscent of many earlier examples of the response to children's literature, such as the perceived threat of fantasy articulated in the nineteenth century, yet it remains powerfully influential in the market for children's fiction. The 'Disneyfication' of story and the desire to provide a unified world-view predominate in the lucrative world of children's fiction.

Series fiction, such as the Hardy Boys and the Sweet Valley High series, may attract the 'kiddy-dollar', but it is the rise of the experimental, multi-voiced, metafictional children's text in the latter half of the twentieth century that declares its debt to postmodern forms of expression. Rather than enslavement to the fear of the effects of technology, heterogeneity and the lack of moral structure, children's literature has become, in some instances, an expression of possibility; embracing the energies of postmodern art, as

> it splices high and low culture, it raids and parodies past art, it questions all absolutes, it swamps reality in a culture of recycled images, it has to do with deconstruction, with consumerism, with television and the information society. . .
>
> (Brooker 1992: 3)

By making use of, rather than being at the mercy of, the postmodern condition, some contemporary children's writers offer powerful positions for their audiences; disrupting expectations of the traditional storytelling modes, and acknowledging children as natural deconstructionist readers. Aidan Chambers, whose work for teenagers continually breaks the boundaries of narrative, sees, in children's literature, the key to understanding these disruptions of power structures.

> I have often wondered why literary theorists haven't yet realised that the best demonstration of almost all they say when they talk about phenomenology or structuralism or deconstruction of any other critical approach can be most clearly and easily demonstrated in children's literature.
>
> (Chambers 1985: 133)

By engaging with the conditions of children in contemporary society, many writers make playful use of postmodern strategies that place children as readers in a powerful position. The extent to which children are now fed by a barrage of fractured images from television and film and are defined by their place in consumer culture can be seen as an influence in recent children's texts. While those books, which are strongly marketed and account for the majority of children's book sales, may be formulaic and lazy, there are also many writers calling attention to the artfulness and relevance of children's texts as a splicing of high and low culture.

Peter Brooker claims that postmodernism is 'a deliberate affront to the decorums and hierarchies of the literary establishment' (Brooker 1992: 2). Although the many philosophers and cultural critics who debate the boundaries of this definition refer to literature, art, film and architecture, they ignore the tendency, in children's literature, to engage in a playful relationship with literary modes in a way that undermines their hierarchical function. While postmodernism concerns itself principally with the production of works from 1950s to the present day, the connection between the contemporary challenges to notions of authoritative discourses and Bakhtin's notion of the *carnivalesque* indicates the historical roots of these tendencies. The use of parody and allusion in Lewis Carroll's Alice books, or the metafictional strategies of MacDonald, E. Nesbit and Mary Norton, already discussed above, suggest that the playfulness and sense of performance inherent in children's literature as a form has always been available. McGillis, in *The Nimble Reader*, claims that those strategies that we now deem postmodern are those which 'entrust authority in the reader' (1996: 176). These strategies, in evidence throughout the history of children's literature, remain reliant on a constructed image of 'the child' as an ideal reader − a Romantic construction.

It is possible to claim that postmodernity derives from the historical situation of late capitalism and the multicultural epoch. Certainly, the ontological anxieties expressed following the Second World War and discussed in Chapter Ten, contribute to a situation for those who write for children, wherein the need to offer a picture of the world 'as it is' must be continually deferred. Fundamental uncertainty about the nature of the physical world and the dislocation of a moral order threatens the kind of message expected in the stories we offer children. The assumption that narrative trustworthiness, authorial control, closure and determinate meaning should be defining characteristics of the less difficult experience of reading children's fiction are challenged by the work of numerous children's authors. John Burningham, Raymond Briggs, David McCauley, Allan and Janet Ahlberg, Jon Scieszka and Lane Smith, Philip Pullman, Paul Zindel, Robert Cormier and Aidan Chambers all incorporate postmodern strategies in their work to challenge expected reader/author relationships.

It is noticeable at once that many of the authors listed are authors and illustrators of picture books or, alternatively, writers for the young adult or teenage market. Many critics, such as Geoff Moss and David Lewis, have commented on the postmodern qualities of the contemporary picture book, and it is striking that this particular form has not been annexed by the cultural critic as an example of a postmodern consciousness in both visual and linguistic terms. While the discussion of *The Stinky Cheese Man and other Fairly Stupid Tales* in Chapter Sixteen offers a more detailed account of one striking example of such a text, it is the frequency with which recent picture books embrace the parodic challenge to dominant narratives and thus call attention to the constructedness of stories, that must be noted here. Allan and Janet Ahlberg, in the Jolly Postman series, for instance, are more restrained in their playful allusions to fairy tales, but share the metafictional strategies that mark the most subversive work of Jon Scieszka and Lane Smith. However, while the Ahlberg's play *within* the fairy-tale world that the illustrations evoke, the American Scieszka and Smith disrupt and subvert the world of fantasy and attempt to undermine the didactic, and thus controlling, force of fairy tales. Their books are, in some ways, parodic and function both as a liberation from the moralistic intentions of fairy stories, and as a postmodern acknowledgement of their cultural currency. *Squids Will Be Squids* (2000) follows this formula: adopting the form of Aesop's fables while, at the same time, warning of the dangers of fables as a form of social critique. By framing their parodic fables with the factual story of Aesop and his death, the authors offer a metafictional gloss which calls attention to the power of stories. Similarly, Babette Cole uses her anarchic illustrations and carnivalesque interest in bodily functions to undermine the power of children's stories to inflect gender norms on their readers. In such books as *Princess Smartypants* (1994) and, more recently, *Hair in Funny Places* (2000), Cole is able to challenge dominant discourses. Although retaining the dominant assumptions about maleness and femaleness, Cole reverses roles and invites her readers, through allusion, to question their own assumptions. Her picture books about puberty and sex also have the power to shock parents and teachers, thereby offering the children who read the books a subversive sense of power over authority.

In other ways, picture books demand a more active, *writerly* engagement from their readers through postmodern narrative strategies. John Burningham, with *Grandpa* (1984) or *Come Away From the Water, Shirley* (1977), offers a plurality of narratives which can connect in a variety of ways. Without a central controlling authorial discourse, the meaning is devolved to the child as a reader. When, at the end of *Grandpa*, the wordless illustration of the chair disrupts our expectations of closure, the reader must interpret, for him/herself, a personal reading. This may be more difficult and less comforting than authorial control, yet it is more enabling, inviting the reader to voice an individual view. Similarly, in *Come Away from the Water, Shirley*, the wordless narrative of Shirley's piratical adventures rub up against the nearly colourless narrative of her parents' experience on the beach and her mother's monologue. The reader must negotiate the multilayered structure of the book and the relationship between the narratives. The experience of reading is made strange and either narrative can dominate. While some readers will be drawn to share in the telling of the wordless narrative, others will find the repressive quality of the mother's influence the most powerful representation of contemporary family life.

The use of the multiple narrative in postmodern fiction is at once performative and generous. While such methods call attention to the construction of the text and challenge the notion of a unified version of events, they also force the reader to engage with the space between the narratives, in order to negotiate a personal version. These openings or gaps reveal the writerly qualities of these texts, sharing the telling with the reader. Maurice Sendak, in *Where the Wild Things Are* (1970), 'plays with the double narrative of picture and text' (Thacker 2001). By removing the narrative for three double pages while Max has his 'wild rumpus', Sendak invites the reader to become the author of fictional events. As the story relates Max's revolt against parental suppression, the narrative disruptions of the authorial relationship and the act of telling are at once subversive and pleasurable.

Many children's writers, and it may not be surprising that writers for teenagers predominate, use similar methods to disrupt the authoritative tendency. Paul Zindel's *The Pigman* (1970) offers a shared narrative between male and female protagonists, while Robert Swindell's *Daz4Zoe* (1992) narrates the same events from the point of view of class in a future society in which only those 'inside' have access to education and, thus, power over language. While one narrative is grammatical and easy to understand, the other is fragmentary and in need of translation. Those texts which decline the position of authority, or refuse to privilege one discourse over the other, suggest a postmodern response to the dislocations at work in contemporary culture. Readers are, thus, invited (particularly those readers on the cusp of adulthood and with a special interest in the play of power) to explore a variety of positions in relation to history or truth.

Aidan Chambers' recent novel, set in both contemporary times and the Second World War, *Postcards from No Man's Land* (2000), uses the multiple narrative to engage the reader in the euthanasia debate while also emphasising the fact that there are different versions that are read as history. Chambers, long a champion of children's literature and its complexity, continually subverts the author/reader relationship in his novels for young people. In *Breaktime* (1978) for instance, he uses self-reflexivity and metafiction to make 'the reader think about how language is being employed to tell a story' (Reynolds 1994: 49). By using shifting narratives, and incorporating the numerous voices of journalism and medical books, for instance, Chambers is able to challenge expectations of a unified text. At the same time, his tendency to tackle taboo subjects, such as homosexuality and euthanasia, stretches the definition of children's literature. With Robert Cormier, author of *The Chocolate War* (1974) and *I Am the Cheese* (1977), Chambers is one of several contemporary authors to suggest a testing of boundaries within children's literature both in terms of subject matter and narrative technique. Blurring the boundaries between what is, or is not, for children invites public debate about society's own role in constructing images of 'the child', and the questioning which feeds back into fiction *for* children.

Changes in the discourses surrounding literature in general also exert an influence on children's literature. The advent of post-structuralist criticism, which accompanied the postmodern trends in art, offers new perspectives from which to think about children's literature. The blurring of the distinction between the popular and the literary, with all of its elitist connotations, suggested ways of considering children's books as a political force within the system of language. Feminist criticism, in particular, gave children's literature critics and theorists the discourses to explore the place of children's books in the hierarchy of culture. The power of these texts to subvert patriarchal ideologies through an engagement with imaginative language offers a new perspective for reading children's literature as part of a wider frame of reference.

The rise of poststructuralist criticism is a decanonising force, challenging the claims for the superiority of high art. The heterogeneity that such a force suggests is at the centre of postmodern experiment in art, and children's writers and illustrators continually make use of the rejection of higher privileged discourses and the breakdown of the division between high culture and popular art. Anthony Browne's visual reference points in books such as *Willy's Pictures* (2000), depend on a familiarity with canonised works of art, and *Changes* (1995), which uses Christian iconography. By interpolating images of his own characters and popular images into these paintings, Browne breaks down the boundaries and provides a sense of play. *Gorilla* (1983), too, pays homage to both Whistler and da Vinci, by presenting both Whistler's Mother and the Mona Lisa as gorillas.

This is not only parody, however, but a way of breaking away from assumptions about readership and the nature of the popular cultural form of children's literature. In *Voices in the Park* (2000), Browne provides multiple narratives, providing a sense of the lack of a unified worldview, to call attention to power structures according to class, but also within adult/child relationships. The surrealism in the illustrations and the use of different typefaces to denote voices in the text invite readers to construct their own narrative of the relationships portrayed in a sophisticated way.

While it has always been true that children's authors often share a joke with the adult reader over the head of the child, Browne, along with many other contemporary writers for children, is more explicit in his invitations to a dual readership. Thus, the ludic, or playful, qualities described above claim a place for the text beyond its restricting definition as a book for children. Raymond Briggs, who uses related forms of parody in *Fungus the Bogeyman* (1977) and a comic-book style to convey complex narratives of loss in, for instance, *The Man* (1992), is another author whose work is marketed for children, but who continually blurs the boundaries of readership. *Ethel and Ernest A True Story* (1998) makes use of the same methods of narration to tell the story of his parents' marriage, yet was marketed only for adults.

The attraction of children's fiction for an adult audience can be seen as part of the postmodern condition. The desire to challenge adult assumptions, to return to (if it ever existed) a playful or original conception of the world can be interpreted as the Romantic anarchism which Brooker (1992) claims is related to postmodern challenges to decorum. There are many examples, particularly in North America, of artful children's books which are bought, almost exclusively, by adults for their own entertainment. Griswold (1997), suggests that this is part of the disappearance, in America, of the 'notion of childhood'. Yet the popularity of children's books in both academic circles and the market reflects 'adult nostalgia for a notion of [childhood's] evanescence, in a twilight period just before its disappearance' (Beckett 1997: 38).

The blurring of boundaries between the child and adult audiences is also evident in the phenomenon of the ubiquitous J.K. Rowling, author of the Harry Potter books. While one could interpret the decision of her canny publishers to issue both children's and adult versions for the first book as a cynical marketing ploy, Rowling's popularity with adults points to an expression of the postmodern epoch. Her books provide a series of compelling adventures and offer a narrative voice that is comforting and controlling at the same time. In many ways, Rowling's books rely on the very assumptions that are challenged by postmodern attitudes. The heroic *Bildungsroman* is devoid of ironic double-voicing and, apart from the occasional aside in the first volume, allows no opportunities for an active engagement with the author. While the books have become darker as Harry grows older, the opposition of good and evil and the confident authorial voice seems to rely on a Romantic model of the child reader as innocent, but in need of controlling narratives. What is more, the strength of the popularity of her books with adults suggests a desire to return to this relationship to fictional text, which is less active and therefore less challenging.

Rather than carnivalising the school story and the adventure narrative, Rowling pays homage and thus offers readers an escape from the experimental and the subversive. While columnists, booksellers and parents rejoice in the fact that children are reading, it must be admitted that the Harry Potter books posit a reader who requires consolation in a difficult world, rather than a reader willing to make his or her own meaning.

Although Rowling's work provides a perspective of real world problems through the lens of the 'fantastic' in a conventional way, subversive invitations to 'play' within the text are more frequently seen in recent children's fiction than in the literature produced for an adult market. While adult literature may deal with social fractures and the interplay of race, class and gender through realism and sensationalism, some of the most challenging children's books make their meaning through playful disruption of the real.

The 'His Dark Materials' trilogy by Philip Pullman (*Northern Lights* 1995, *The Subtle Knife* 1997 and *The Amber Spyglass* 2000), encompasses religion, quantum physics and the disruption of moral certainties to suggest a return to the dual readership of nineteenth-century children's literature. Refusing to 'talk down', Pullman constructs an implied reader capable of engaging with both the force of the plot and the indeterminacy of meaning. While Pullman has argued that only children's fiction can deal with the large themes with which he wishes to engage (Hunt and Lenz 2001: 122), the market is troubled by their status as children's fiction. The recent appearance of the final volume on the Booker 'longlist' has contributed to recent debates about children's literature. Pullman is clearly interested in questioning the boundaries society draws, relying on an estimation of children as readers reminiscent of George MacDonald's visionary ideas. The discussion of Pullman's *Clockwork* which follows, calls attention to his willingness to question the act of telling stories to children, and to look back to the origins of the folk and fairy tale in a postmodern and playful way.

McGillis, in *The Nimble Reader* (1996) calls attention to the originality of Chris Van Allsburg's *The Mysteries of Harris Burdick* (1984), which offers a number of evocative illustrations accompanied by equally mysterious captions. The lost stories, of which these artefacts are supposedly the remnants, offer powerful positions for the reader and the indeterminacy of meaning proclaims the text as decidedly postmodern. This boundary-breaking quality of the book challenges the expectations of the relationship between author/artist and reader/viewer in a similar way to the most experimental adult fiction of the late twentieth century. In particular, the use of multiple narratives in such novels as Morrison's *Beloved* (1987), or magic realism in the work of Angela Carter or Gabriel García Márquez, plays with the distinctions between reality and fantasy and unsettles the power structures of language and culture. Such disruptions are subversive and challenge the domination of patriarchal structures reflected in any colonial relationship, to which the adult/child relationship can be compared.

The lure of the feminine narrative and the possibilities of engaging with fiction in an open and writerly way, seen throughout the history of children's literature, are offered by such books as these. Fluidity and indeterminacy of meaning, lack of closure and play with language all contribute to children's literature as a revolutionary force.

The use of the carnivalesque to express a resistance to controlling narratives and the open invitation of so many recent children's books, rely on the idea of a reader who will come to the book with an inherently 'innocent' response. It is the pre-social, anti-elitist aspects of Bakhtin's notion of the carnivalesque which suggests its relevance to children's literature. The challenges offered by mass cultural forms to dominant and powerful discourses are familiar in the work of many of the writers discussed in this book. A writerly engagement with language, and the suggestion of an ability to make meaning suggests a Romantic sensibility that touches on the feminine, *imaginary*, roots of creativity, and thereby subverts the dominance of masculine order. Understanding through story appears to be, throughout history, an essential capability and an essential desire, yet it is the ontological uncertainty of contemporary society which makes this desire more urgent. The power of 'play and reconciliation' which Brooker claims for postmodernism (1992: 14) is clearly articulated throughout the history of children's books.

The maternal, feminine roots of children's writing can be seen to shift and change in response to social realities, yet they retain and develop a sense of resistance to controlling and dominant power structures and can thus be considered an ally to postmodernist responses to the contemporary culture and society. Throughout the influence of the prevailing patriarchal discourses of the nineteenth century, these roots retained their influence and found expression in children's texts, often as a challenge to the conventions of bourgeois realism. Despite a gradual loss of confidence in the authorial position as perceiver of truths and authority, these texts were, at heart, subversive and upheld the revolutionary tendency of art. The relatively minor status of literature for children and its close connection with mothering and the feminine may have masked its importance as an undermining force, but the breaking of cultural boundaries, motivated by poststructuralist theory, has allowed the full influence of these texts to be appreciated. The strategies which we now name as postmodern are familiar to readers of children's literature throughout its history, yet it is only recently that we can recognise the central role of that literature – to maintain a voice of challenge to the authoritarian voices which seek to control and enslave.

Many critics point to the truth that literary writers were strongly influenced by the books they read as children, and it is perhaps the ability of literature to either colonise or liberate that characterises that influence. The fascination with 'the child' who, since the Romantic movement, has affected, and been affected by, the way in which we understand the relationship between the individual and society is, perhaps, only a projection of our need to tell stories about ourselves that allow us to live. As our perception of the function of these stories changes, so our awareness of the power of narrative exchanges is transformed from certainty surrounding the author's function to an admission of the power of the reader. This shift in perception of power in the author/reader relationship, central to the construction of children's literature as a form, demands an understanding of the ways in which the texts written for children throughout history express that desire for stories that liberate.

The chapters that follow examine more closely the power of children's books to perform that liberating function. The parodic and metafictional strategies employed by Pullman and Scieszka provide narratives that defamiliarise the experience of reading. Their complexity and the challenges they offer emphasise the extent to which children's literature continues to engage with contemporary literary movements. The perspectives offered throughout this book are derived from an understanding of literature as a form which shifts in response to cultural and aesthetic change.

Finally, the aim of this book has been, in some senses, to combat the absence of these children's texts from this way of understanding literary history. The revolutionary capacity of much of the children's literature discussed within these pages is controlled by virtue of their marginalised status as 'only' children's books. The hope is that the perspectives offered here will further our understanding, not only of the place of children's literature within a critical history of literature, but an insight into the ways in which readers are constructed within that history.

Chapter 15

Clockwork

A fairy tale for a postmodern time

Philip Pullman's postmodern text *Clockwork* (1997), is a fairy tale in which Pullman produces a moral critique of contemporary Western society. The tale works as a metaphor depicting the triumph of human compassion over the destructive and selfish drives of capitalism, which threaten to produce a mechanistic and loveless society. In Pullman's tale, society is driven by selfish inhumane Faustian desires which eradicate the most human quality of love. *Clockwork*, however, is not a simple didactic moral tale, but a complex postmodern text. The narrative works in a metafictive way in which it 'enacts or performs what it wishes to say about narrative' (Currie 1998: 52) and also mirrors the moral intention of the text. The reader is engaged in a narrative structure which both parallels the mechanistic drive of society, whilst actively involving the individual reader as a maker of meaning. This is possible through the postmodern nature of the text.

Structurally the text comprises a number of narrative frames. The principal voice is that of the narrator, who acts as the overarching storyteller and also as an omniscient narrator. The comments of the narrator are embedded in the text as commentary on the characters and as obvious physical frames inserted into the text in which additional moral and didactic comment is made, and 'information' given. The other narrative voice is that of the character Fritz, a young storyteller, whose tale frames the events experienced by the other characters. The reader is made highly conscious of the structure of the narrative throughout the text. Such an awareness is typical of postmodern writing.

The reading experience begins with an extract from the text. It is an untitled section which foregrounds the activity of storytelling:

'I'm looking forward to this story, even if it does make my hair stand on end.'
'What is it called?'
'It's called –' said Fritz, with a nervous glance at Karl – 'it's called "Clockwork".'

(Pullman 1997)

When the same passage is reread a little later, as part of the narrative itself, the effect is reminiscent of Italo Calvino's postmodern novel *If On A Winter's Night A Traveller* (Calvino 1982), where the reader is returned to the beginning of a story a number of times through the novel. The sense of beginning and rebeginning is continued in the Preface, 'Clockwork', which follows the extract and title page. It begins 'In the old days, when this story took place' (Pullman 1997: 7).

The question entering the reader's mind is 'which story?' – the one to be told by Fritz, or the narrator? Or will they be one and the same? The reader is therefore engaged in questions of narrative construction.

The Preface sets the time period for the story, 'In the old days', and enters into a discussion on the nature of clockwork. Pullman uses the notion of clockwork as a metafictive device, comparing the workings of clockwork to storytelling. Each element of the text is interrelated like a component in a clockwork mechanism. He states that once the narrative preparations have been made the story will run like clockwork to its own conclusion. There is an ironic and playful position here, since the writer/narrator is also the creator of the text, and could make changes. The metafictive Preface also acts as a metaphorical expression of Pullman's philosophical and moral position in the text. He makes the observation that when technology has become highly advanced, 'like a watch run by a solar panel', it may be wondrously efficient, but defies the individual having any influence. This is an implicit critique of contemporary society, where the individual is negated by the sophisticated development of systems. The reader is being prepared for Pullman's moral argument which develops through the text, i.e. that society has become mechanical at the sacrifice of humanity. By setting the story in a less sophisticated past age, the fictional period of 'fairy tale', Pullman produces circumstances where there is still the possibility for individual moral action to take place. The playfulness of the Preface is balanced by a certain sense of foreboding and menace, for this will be a story to frighten as well as entertain. Within a short, witty and self-contained preface Pullman has set the emotional and moral expectations of the reading experience to be played out through the text.

Part One begins the story again: 'Once upon a time (when time ran by clockwork)' (Pullman 1997: 11). The text is already working on a self-referential basis, including playfully making puns, taking the reader back to previous parts of the text. This beginning is in the traditional mode of fairy tale. The 'strange event' which 'took place in a little German town' (Pullman 1997: 11) is set in an unspecified past, where, as it were, all European tales take place. Intertextual resonances are also set up with the work of the Grimm brothers through the reference to Germany. The focus of conversation in the inn is the event of the following day when Karl the apprentice clockmaker is to complete his apprenticeship by presenting his new clockwork figure to be included in the great clock tower at Glockenheim. The reader is also reminded here of Hoffman's tale 'The Automaton', which focuses on a clockwork figure. At this point in the text Pullman inserts the first illustrated framed page which breaks the conventions of a traditional seamless text. The reader is given factual information on the Glockenheim clock, which suggests a context of reality, backed up by the authoritative assertion of the narrator who concludes the section with the words 'There never was a clock like it, I promise'. The phrase punningly suggests that no clock has ever existed of the ilk of the Glockenheim piece, and also that there never was such a clock. There is a slippage of meaning here. Fact and fantasy are intermingled in the mind of the reader, setting a challenge to the trustworthiness of language and the nature of reality. Pullman is positing a postmodern philosophical position about the nature of reality.

Karl, the apprentice, is anxious and ill-tempered; the reader suspects that he has been unable to fulfil his task. The topic of conversation switches to the other young man, Fritz, the novelist, who is going to read his new story that evening. The atmosphere of foreboding and tension escalates as the group discuss the frightening nature of Fritz's ghost stories. Temperamentally Fritz is the opposite of Karl, who is full of savage bitterness as he contemplates the embarrassing failure of his years of apprenticeship. The traditional fairy-tale mode of the use of oppositions is seemingly set up: Karl as the evil figure, Fritz as the good. The assumption is that

Fritz is able to create freely, whilst Karl's struggle is due to an 'artistic temperament'. Pullman's framed insertion here draws attention to the dedication required to be an artist, that real talent is also allied to hard work, rather than ethereal creative happenstance. The tone of the narrator's insertion is scornful and didactic. The manner is akin to that of the omniscient narrative style of nineteenth-century novels, where direct comment was included in the text in a seemingly unconscious manner. Here it is consciously inserted to draw attention in a dialogic manner, to the 'conversation' in the inn, and to add weight to the moral comment which is being made. The central point is that writing is as much work as creating a clockwork figure. The narrator also draws attention to the constructedness of the text, by making reference to difficulties Fritz will experience a few pages into the future. Fritz has written his story from a dream, and only has the first part. The reader is being initiated both into the difficulties of writing, and into the moral position that fulfilment comes only from dedicated hard work and planning allied to inspiration, not merely from dreams. There is an implicit invitation in the construction of the text, for the reader to project their own tale about Fritz's efforts to overcome his weakness, and triumph as a great writer.

Fritz's story is narrated to the reader, so that one gains the vicarious experience of listening to a storyteller. He declares that his story is not about Karl, nor the clock, but happens to be called 'Clockwork'. The reader is engaged in a text which involves a self-referential puzzle-solving challenge, that is, to work out how the pieces of the narrative will fit together, for the narrator has pointed out previously that 'although each person saw a different part, no-one saw the whole of it' (Pullman 1997: 11). The only person who has the overview is the reader – as far as the narrator will allow. Pullman is combining the genres of fairy tale, where the reader is a passive recipient, and detective fiction, where the reader is active in solving the puzzle. (Phillip Pullman has written detective fiction for children, for example *The Ruby in the Smoke* [1994].) He is also stating his awareness of the postmodern position, that there is no one fixed truth, for the contemporary understanding of consciousness and society is about multiplicity and difference.

Fritz's strange tale is told as though it were history, asking the listeners to recall events which occurred 'a few years ago'. The effect is that the fantastic and uncanny proceedings are given the status of reality. Prince Otto dies whilst on a winter hunting trip with his son, returning as a mechanised corpse because his heart has been removed and replaced by a clockwork mechanism, enabling the dead Prince to drive home the sledge carrying his child. There is a direct allusion here to the famous quotation from Thomas Carlyle's nineteenth-century essay 'Signs of the Times', where Carlyle states that 'Men are grown mechanical in head and in heart, as well as in hand' (Carlyle 1971: 67). Carlyle's essay, and this phrase in particular, was a warning to Victorian society of the dangers of industrialisation and capitalism. The moral of Pullman's story echoes that very warning throughout the continuation of the tale.

Confused by the spectacle of the princely-driven sledge the courtiers turn in innocence to Dr Kalmenius, the master clock-maker, for an answer to this macabre mystery. The Doctor is known to live a strange life, and rumoured to experiment on dead bodies. The narrative framed insertion tells the reader that Kalmenius makes uncannily life-like clockwork figures. Intertextual allusions to Mary Shelley's *Frankenstein* are suggested by the inception of Fritz's tale as a dream, echoing Mary Shelley's experience of writing her novel. The suggestion is that Dr Kalmenius, like Dr Frankenstein, seeks the secret of life, and is prepared to make a monster to pursue his ambitions. Kalmenius is described as being a menacing monk-like figure, whose expression was 'full of savage curiosity'. Reality and fantasy are brought together before the group of listeners when Dr Kalmenius proves to be a living person, by entering the inn. Karl is taken up by Kalmenius as an accomplice in his dark arts. Kalmenius is a megalomaniac. Karl wants an easy way to satisfy his ambition, and emulate the power of his mentor. Pullman's narrative voice becomes clearly morally didactic from this point. The frame emphasises the moral comment, and enables Pullman to make moral links with contemporary behaviour, such as the obsession with the lottery as a way of wishfully solving all problems. Karl's wish is fulfilled in the form of a murderous clock-work knight, aptly named Sir Ironsoul. The knight is activated by the word 'devil' and stopped by whistling a special tune. The Faustian allusion is clear.

At the darkest point in the text, attention is drawn to the land-lord's daughter Gretel (her name bringing to mind the story of 'Hansel and Gretel'). She voices a sympathetic and humanitarian concern for the young Prince Florian, the child brought back by his dead father. Her kindness and goodness are stressed by the narrator. A further episode in the history of Prince Otto's family

is unfolded by the narrator, who is the only one to know this part
of the story. The reader is being shifted back and forth in time,
piecing together the complexities of the narrative. We are told that
Prince Otto is maniacally consumed by the desire for the continuation of his line. A child is born finally, not of love, but of wishes.
The child dies, and is taken by Otto to Dr Kalmenius. Prince Otto
requests that Kalmenius make a clockwork child. The request is
granted and Kalmenius creates a wondrously life-like figure whom
they name Florian. The figure works well for five years, but then
begins to show signs of running down. On returning to Kalmenius
the only solution suggested is that the figure should have a human
heart. Rather than give his life for his son Prince Otto is prepared
to sacrifice the heart of his servant; however, foiled by fate, he has
to give his own heart. Even at this point it is done for pride, ambition and notions of power, rather than love. The story unwinds like
clockwork, returning the reader to the first episode recounted as
Fritz's story.

Pullman's Preface to *Clockwork* guides the reader in the mode of
reading, by using the metaphor of the mechanism of clockwork
with all its related parts as a unified mode of movement. As the
narrative is drawn to a conclusion the fragments of the story are
pieced together by the reader. Karl places the mechanical Prince
Florian in the tower as his apprentice piece. He is then killed by
Sir Ironsoul, providing a fitting end for a selfish and soulless young
fellow. The mechanism for this is that Karl is startled by the cat
Putzi, whom he has ill-treated. Putzi has been present as part of
the scenery throughout. Gretel is determined to ensure that Fritz
finishes what he has begun, that is, that he should finish his story.
Ironically it is she who completes the story by comforting the
mechanical Prince and bringing him to life with her unselfish love,
which carries no wish of self-reward.

Pullman's text combines a strong moral message with a witty,
ironic style and a tense exciting story. The postmodern style of narration enables Pullman to be most effective within a short, compact
text, where the involvement of the reader is paramount. If a morally
grounded work is to be effective, then the reader must be an active
participant, and absorb the moral viewpoint. Philip Pullman has
proven that *Clockwork* need not be a mechanical experience.

Chapter 16

A postmodern reflection on the genre of fairy tale

The Stinky Cheese Man and Other Fairly Stupid Tales

Deborah Stevenson identifies Jon Scieszka and Lane Smith's *The Stinky Cheese Man* (Scieszka and Smith 1993), as 'the classic postmodern picture book' (Stevenson 1994: 32–4). The text is a postmodern reflection on the picture book as an artefact and the fairy tale as a genre. In conventional texts both the book as a physical form and the fairy tale are constructed about conventions which are unquestioningly accepted by the reader. Scieszka and Smith disrupt the expectations of the reader through the self-reflexive narrative structure and visual style of *The Stinky Cheese Man*. They make the conventions obvious, and question them in a ludic and stimulating manner. The reader is consistently active as the maker of meaning throughout *The Stinky Cheese Man*. The implied reader is required to draw upon a knowledge of books, narrative structure and fairy tales in order to construct meaning in the gaps between the traditional forms and Scieszka and Smith's postmodern text. *The Stinky Cheese Man* contains nine parodic rewritings of fairy tales, and combines other verbal narratives running through the text circulating about Jack the Narrator and Chicken Licken; there are also multiple layers of meaning communicated through the illustrations. It is a complex text. The intention of this discussion is to focus upon selected elements dealing with the book as a physical form, the narrative structure and a consideration of the revisioning of certain tales to demonstrate and discuss the postmodern nature of the work. Since there are slight variations between the hardback and paperback editions, the areas of discussion are those which are common to both.

The first endpaper of *The Stinky Cheese Man* immediately disrupts the conventions of the picture book. Normally the reader would expect a double-page illustration which would present a visual key to the text, for example, a map in the case of the Ahlberg's *Each, Peach, Pear Plum*. However, Scieszka and Smith elect to introduce the reader to the dialogic nature of the work through the use of striking typeface to represent an antagonistic discussion between The Little Red Hen and Jack the Narrator. The dialogue occupies most of the page. The dialogue of the Little Red Hen is in large red bold typeface. Jack's words are in a more moderate black, and slightly smaller. The contrast between their personalities is evident in the visual representation of their words. The Little Red Hen speaks in the linguistic style of her fairy-tale character as though she has no pattern of discourse outside of the demands of that narrative:

> 'I have found a kernel of wheat,' said the Little Red Hen. 'Now who will help me plant this wheat? Where is that lazy dog? Where is that lazy cat? Where is that lazy mouse?'
> (Scieszka and Smith 1993: endpaper)

She is demanding, and seemingly in control until she is forcibly interrupted by the following: 'Wait a minute. Hold everything. You can't tell your story right here. This is the endpaper. The book hasn't even started yet' (Scieszka and Smith 1993: endpaper).

The voice of the narrator unusually draws attention to the publishing conventions of the construction of a book as an artefact. Jack introduces himself as the narrator and states: 'I'm a very busy guy trying to put a book together. Now, why don't you just disappear for a few pages. I'll call when I need you' (Scieszka and Smith 1993: endpaper).

Jack is not tied to a particular pattern of discourse as is the Little Red Hen. His fairy-tale character in Jack and the Beanstalk is constructed around his actions rather than his words. In the context of narrator Jack assumes an equally active approach: as he made the beanstalk grow (albeit by chance) he is about to make the book 'grow'. He makes his narrative role obvious. For Jack, as a postmodern narrator, the construction of the text is a physical task. The reader thus gains a sense of the book as a physical entity rather than a linguistic and visual representation divorced from the actualities of production. The physicality of the text is reinforced by Jack's closing words: 'Listen Hen – forget the wheat. Here comes the Title Page!' (Scieszka and Smith 1993: endpaper) as though the page is forcibly descending upon them. The notion of the text takes on a reality which dispels any sentimentality or mystique about artistic production. This approach is contradictory to the unreality of the conventions of the genre of fairy tale. The literary fairy tale produced by writers from the Romantic tradition, such as Hans Andersen, would have been perceived as having been born of the imagination with no reference to the physicality of the process.

The illustration to the endpaper dialogue between the Little Red Hen and Jack emphasises the character of the hen as demanding, repetitive and not very bright. Here the characters are more complex than the simple outline expected in fairy tales. The intention of the fairy tale is to broadly represent a moral position: in consequence the characters can be readily associated with their representational value, for example the poor young male trickster who defeats the rich wicked giant. The illustrations reflect the complexity of character working as an integral part of the text. They are all full colour, bold and comically grotesque in style with a presence which demands that the reader pay attention to the pictures. In the opening endpaper section the Little Red Hen and Jack are pictured in the bottom right hand corner. The picture illustrates the intensity of their discussion with the Little Red Hen shouting at Jack, who glares at her whilst trying to block her words by putting his fingers in his ears. Jack has a saw-toothed mouth which emphasises his aggressive stance toward this overbearing, red-faced loudmouthed chicken. These are certainly not sentimental or Romanticised images.

Even with such a short experience of the book the reader has already dispelled the normal associations expected of the genre of fairy tale. *The Stinky Cheese Man* is an energetic, funny, parodic text, whereas fairy tales are not usually associated with humour. They may have a trickster who could be regarded as mildly comic, or scenes of slapstick humour, such as chains of characters unfortunately joined together, as in the Golden Goose however, what the fairy tale normally lacks is verbal humour and wit, which requires the interaction and intelligence of the reader to make the joke. Jack's discourse reflects a quick wit, and the turn of phrase more readily associated with the street dialogue of New York or Glasgow than the collected fairy tales of the Grimm Brothers. The opening dialogue between Jack and the Hen has produced a narrative which will appear intermittently through the text and involve other characters. This, in itself, disrupts the expectation of a collection of fairy tales, for the presence of a narrative involving the narrator and other characters is foreign to the narrative style of fairy tales. Paradoxically what the reader can expect is a sense of narrative unpredictability. The introduction reinforces the reader's expectation of unpredictability because the reader is told that 'The stories in this book are almost Fairy Tales. But not quite. The stories in this book are Fairly Stupid Tales' (Scieszka and Smith 1993: Introduction). The pun implies that the reader can expect comic twists, linguistic play, and the awareness of language and form typical of postmodernism.

The first three tales in *The Stinky Cheese Man*, 'The Princess and the Bowling Ball', 'The Really Ugly Duckling' and 'The Other Frog Prince' work on a similar principle, resolving to the real rather than the magical and the ideal. The ironic play on the form is that the genres of realism and the fantasy of fairy tale are polar opposites. Scieszka and Smith deconstruct the fantasy by resolving the problem at the centre of the tale with a rational rather than a fantastic solution. Two of the three tales in the first triad have been selected for discussion: 'The Really Ugly Duckling' and 'The Other Frog Prince'.

'The Really Ugly Duckling' is a revisioning of Hans Andersen's literary fairy tale, 'The Ugly Duckling'. The focus of this discussion is on the Scieszka and Smith parody with general reference to the Andersen text. 'The Really Ugly Duckling' is a condensed rewriting of the Andersen story which runs to approximately four thousand words (Andersen 1959), whilst the Scieszka and Smith parody is told in about one hundred words plus two full page illustrations. The Scieszka and Smith illustrations are integral to the reading of the text, as will be discussed below. Andersen's story is one of the trials of a cygnet who is hatched out by a duck. The tale is one of mistaken self-identity, and self-discovery through trial and tribulation as the Ugly Duckling engages in a *Bildungsroman* series of adventures before he can recognise himself as an elegant and beautiful swan. He admires the swans during his stages as an ungainly cygnet, whilst believing himself to be a misfit, a rejected and persecuted duckling who is ugly. The dénouement in the Andersen story is an emotional and sentimental release from the pains of self-emergence and mistaken identity. Scieszka and Smith's truncated tale removes description and the protracted trials for the young bird, whilst retaining the fact that he is a misfit with aspirations equal to the Andersen character:

Everyone used to say, 'What a nice looking bunch of ducks –
all except that one. Boy, he's really ugly.' The really ugly duckling heard these people, but he didn't care. He knew that one
day he would probably grow up to be a swan and bigger and
better looking than anything in the pond.

(Scieszka and Smith 1993: 12)

As Peter Hunt pointed out in a conversation on this text, the reader
is forced to pause here because of the page turn, which adds to the
comic power of the piece. On turning the page the reader discovers
that unfortunately the dreams of the ugly duckling are short-lived,
for 'As it turned out, he was just a really ugly duckling. And he
grew up to be just a really ugly duck. The End' (Scieszka and Smith
1993: 13). There is no romantic image of a white swan to accom-
pany the text, but the grotesque caricature of a really ugly duck.

The Scieszka and Smith revisioning removes the Romantic
dreams of the ugly duckling and confronts both the duckling and
the reader with the unsentimental reality. The type face for the
revelation is large, bold and black. The humour is dependent upon
intertextuality, for the laughter is generated by the gaps between
the two tales in both the endings of the stories and the narrative
styles, and by the gap between the projected image of an elegant
swan engendered by readings of the Andersen tale, and the comically grotesque illustrations of Scieszka and Smith. Andersen's
text is elaborate, and descriptive, compared with the brusque and
colloquial tone of Scieszka and Smith's parody. The potential harshness of the postmodern version is alleviated by two grotesquely
comic and zany illustrations which elicit a cathartic response from
the reader. The exaggerated and bizarre form of the saw-toothed
ugly duckling is surrounded by realist drawings of the heads of
ducks and drakes as they peer at this apparition of 'duckness'.
Scieszka and Smith are writing and illustrating against the model
of Andersen's Romanticism. There is no ideal transformation in
their postmodern revision. In their carnivalesque reversal the ugly
duckling does not become a swan, the prince of birds, but remains
the zany outcast, the other. The convention of transformation so
essential to the tradition of the fairy tale has been supplanted
by the removal of the sublime experience, the achievement of the
ideal. The postmodern perspective recognises that we cannot become
ideal selves, idealised forms, for there are realities which have to be
accepted.

'The Other Frog Prince' is a parodic version of the traditional tale, 'The Frog Prince'. It is the story of a mischievous frog who gains a kiss from the princess by pretending that he is a bewitched handsome prince in the guise of a frog who can be released from the spell by her act. Here the illustration is a combination of a scientific annotated drawing realistically depicting the multiplicity of insects fallen prey to the frog's sticky tongue before he was kissed by the unwitting and gullible princess. The frog's tongue is exaggeratedly long. The princess does not appear in the illustration. The reader has to imagine her beauty. The focus is on the reality of the situation with the frog. The ironic suggestion being made is that had the princess not believed in the magical solutions available in fairy tales then she would not have fallen victim to the frog. Scieszka and Smith thereby create multiple layers of intertextual reference. There is the conventional position of readings against extant texts: in addition 'The Other Frog Prince' also positions the frog as gaining by his use of the fairy story as a referent in order to dupe the princess.

The metafictive process of reading involved in *The Stinky Cheese Man* departs from the conventions of fairy tale, that is the 'realism' of the form of the genre, and foregrounds the authors and the reader in inventing and receiving the fiction. The narratives in *The Stinky Cheese Man* are ironically positioned in realism rather than fantasy. What the implied reader discovers by their absence are the hidden conventions of fairy tale and narrative construction. The artificiality of the fairy tale is dispelled by exposure. Scieszka and Smith's use of the form of the picture book which works on the interaction between text and pictures is also an integral part of this process of exposure. The postmodern reader has to be active, and adaptable to the demands of the narrative. The tale of 'Little Red Running Shorts' and the interaction with the illustration emphasises the unpredictability of the postmodern world as represented through this playful literary parallel. Jack the narrator runs into problems in terms of narrative construction, for he gives a resumé of their story, and therefore removes the necessity of Little Red Running Shorts and the Wolf making their contribution. They see no need to repeat the piece, whereas Jack the Narrator has dedicated the following three pages to their tale. In the following disagreement the two errant characters walk out leaving white figure-shaped spaces in the illustration. Jack has been unreliable as a narrator because he told their story when he should not have done, and the characters are unreliable because they refuse to appear when they should. Jack Zipes in his introduction to his anthology of western fairy tales *Spells of Enchantment* observes that 'both the oral and the literary forms of the fairy tale are grounded in history' (Zipes 1992: xi). Jon Scieszka and Lane Smith's *The Stinky Cheese Man* is a post-modern text grounded in the 'history' of fairy tales, otherwise it could not work, for it is dependent upon the traditional stories for its own meaning. In conclusion, *The Stinky Cheese Man* is a post-modern collection of fairy tales for a postmodern time which creates a postmodern reader.

Bibliography

The bibliography has been selected to provide the reader of children's literature with a sound background to the field, and to the selected texts in this book. Although the work in the field is growing, there is still a very uneven distribution of attention given to authors, so some areas may seem particularly well provided for, whilst in others the criticism is sparse.

The selection of texts also offers a springboard into other areas of reading. Works on literary theory and literary movements have been included to enable the reader to develop a knowledge of children's literature within the context of general literary criticism. Significant journals and websites are also listed.

Abrams, M.H. (1993) *A Glossary of Literary Terms*, 6th edn, London: Harcourt Brace College Publishers.
—— (1999) *A Glossary of Literary Terms*, 7th edn, London: Harcourt Brace College Publishers.
Alcott, L.M. (1891) *Louisa May Alcott: her life, letters and journals*, Boston: Roberts.
—— (1994 [1868]) *Little Women*, (ed.) V. Anderson, London: Puffin.
Alderson, B. (ed.) (1995) Charles Kingsley *The Water-Babies*, Oxford: Oxford World's Classics.
Andersen, H. (1959) *Hans Andersen's Fairy Tales: A Selection*, Oxford: Oxford University Press.
Anderson, Valerie (1994) (ed.) *Louisa May Alcott: Little Women*, Oxford: Oxford University Press.
Avery, Gillian (1994) *Behold the Child: American Children and Their Books 1621–1922*, London: Bodley Head.
Barrie, J.M. (1987 [1911]) *Peter Pan*, New York: Henry Holt and Co.
Barry, P. (1995) *Beginning Theory: An Introduction to Literary and Cultural Theory*, Manchester: Manchester University Press.

Barthes, R. (1975) *The Pleasure of the Text*, London: Jonathan Cape.

Baum, L.F. (1994 [1900]) *The Wonderful Wizard of Oz* in M. Gardner and R. Nye (eds) *The Wizard of Oz and Who He Was*, East Lansing: Michigan State University Press.

Bearne, E., Styles, M. and Watson, V. (1992) *After Alice*, London: Cassell Academic.

—— (1994) *The Prose and the Passion: Children and Their Reading*, London: Cassell Academic.

Beckett, S. (ed.) (1997) *Reflections of Change: Children's Literature Since 1945*, Westport: Greenwood Press.

Beer, G. (2000) *Darwin's Plots: Evolutionary Narrative in Darwin, George Eliot and Nineteenth-century Fiction*, 2nd edn, Cambridge: Cambridge University Press.

Bennett, A. and Royle, N. (1995) *An Introduction to Literature, Criticism and Theory*, Hemel Hempstead: Prentice Hall/Harvester Wheatsheaf.

Bergsten, S. (1978) *Mary Poppins and Myth*, Stockholm: Almquist & Wiksell International.

Bixler, P. (1984) *Frances Hodgson Burnett*, Boston: Twayne Publishers.

Bloom, H. (1987) *Lewis Carroll*, New York: Chelsea House.

Boston, L. (1976 [1954]) *The Children of Green Knowe*, London: Puffin.

Bradbury, M. and Temperley, H. (eds) (1998) *Introduction to American Studies*, 3rd edn, London and New York: Longman.

Bratton, J.S. (1981) *The Impact of Victorian Fiction*, London: Croom Helm.

—— (ed.) (1990) Ballantyne, J. *Coral Island*, Oxford: Oxford University Press.

Bristow, E. (1991) *Empire Boys: Adventures in a Man's World*, London: HarperCollins.

Brooker, P. (1992) *Modernism/Postmodernism*, London: Longman.

Burnett, F.H. (1963 [1905]) *The Little Princess*, Harmondsworth: Penguin.

—— (1987 [1911]) *The Secret Garden*, Oxford: Oxford University Press.

Butler, F. (1972) 'From fantasy to reality: Ruskin's *King of the Golden River*, St George's Guild, and Ruskin, Tennessee', *Children's Literature* 1: 62–73.

Butts, D. (1997) 'How children's literature changed: what happened in the 1840s', *The Lion and the Unicorn: A Critical Journal of Children's Literature*, 21: 153–62.

—— (ed.) (1992) *Stories and Society: Children's Literature in its Social Context*, London: Macmillan.

Cadogan, M. and Craig, P. (1986) *You're A Brick, Angela!*, London: Gollancz.

Calvino, I. (1982) *If On A Winter's Night A Traveller*, New York: Harcourt Brace.

Carlyle, T. (1971 [1829]) *Selected Writings* 'Signs of the Times', Harmondsworth: Penguin Books.

Carpenter, H. (1985) *Secret Gardens: a Study of the Golden Age of Children's Literature,* London: Allen & Unwin.

Carroll, D. (1995) 'Pollution, defilement and the art of decomposition', in K. Clarke (ed.), (1991) *John Ruskin: Selected Writings,* London: Penguin.

Carroll, L. (1992 [1864]) *Alice in Wonderland,* 2nd edn, (ed.) D. Gray, London: W.W. Norton and Company.

Chambers, A. (1985) *Booktalk,* London: The Bodley Head.

Childs, P. (2000) *Modernism,* London: Routledge.

Clark, B.L. (1989) 'A portrait of the artist as a little woman', *Children's Literature* 17: 81–97.

Clark, K. (ed.) (1991) *John Ruskin: Selected Writings,* London: Penguin Classics.

Cohen, M. (1995) *Lewis Carroll: A Biography,* London: Macmillan.

Colloms, B. (1975) *Charles Kingsley: The Lion of Eversley,* London: Constable.

Coveney, P. (1957) *Poor Monkey: The Child in Literature,* London: Rockliff.

—— (1967) *The Image of Childhood,* London: Penguin.

Cullinan, B.E. (ed.) (2001) *The Continuum Encyclopaedia of Children's Literature,* London: Continuum International Publishing Group.

Currie, M. (1998) *Postmodern Narrative Theory,* London: Macmillan.

Day, A. (1995) *Romanticism,* London: Routledge.

Dentith, S. (2000) *Parody,* London: Routledge.

Docherty, T. (ed.) *Postmodernism: A Reader,* Hemel Hempstead: Harvester Wheatsheaf.

Donovan, E.B. (1994) 'Reading for profit and for pleasure: *Little Women* and The Story of a Bad Boy', *The Lion and the Unicorn: A Critical Journal of Children's Literature* 18.2: 143–53.

Doonan, J. (1983) 'Talking pictures: a new look at Hansel and Gretel,' *Signal* 42, September: 123–31.

Dowling, L. (1996) 'The Decadent and the New Woman in the 1890s', in L. Pykett (ed.) *Reading Fin de Siècle Fictions,* London: Longman.

Draper, E.D. and Koralek, J. (eds) (1999) *Lively Oracle: a Centennial Celebration of P.L.Travers, Creator of Mary Poppins,* New York: Larson Publications.

Dusinberre, J. (1999) *Alice to the Lighthouse. Children's Books and Radical Experiments in Art,* London: Palgrave (formerly Macmillan).

Eagleton, T. (1983) *Literary Theory: An Introduction,* Oxford: Basil Blackwell.

Egoff, S., Stubbs, G.T. and Ashley, L.F. (eds) (1969) *Only Connect,* Canada: Oxford University Press.

Eldridge, C.C. (1996) *The Imperial Experience: from Carlyle to Forster,* London: Macmillan.

Emerson, R.W. (1998 [1836]) 'Nature' in Baym *et al.* (eds) *Norton Anthology of American Literature,* Volume 1, NewYork: W.W. Norton.

—— (1998 [1841]) 'Self-Reliance' in Baym *et al.* (eds) *Norton Anthology of American Literature*, Volume 1, New York: W.W. Norton.

Faulkner, P. (1986) *The Modernist Reader*, London: Chrysalis Books.

Fishkin, S. (1998) *Lighting Out For The Territory*, New York: Oxford University Press.

Foster, S. and Simons, J. (1995) *What Katy Read*, London: Macmillan.

Furst, L.R. (1992) *Realism*, Harlow: Longman.

Gardner, M. (ed.) (2000) *The Annotated Alice: the Definitive Edition*, New York: Norton.

Gardner, M. and Nye, R. (1994) 'The Royal Historian of Oz' in M. Gardner and R. Nye (eds) *The Wizard of Oz and Who He Was*, East Lansing: Michigan State University Press.

Gardner, M. and Nye, R. (eds) (1994) *The Wizard of Oz and Who He Was*, East Lansing: Michigan State University Press.

Gilead, S. (1987) 'Liminality and Antiliminality in Charlotte Bronte's Novels: Shirley reads Jane Eyre', *Texas Studies in Literature and Language* 29.3: 302–22.

Gilmour, R. (1993) *The Victorian Period: The Intellectual and Cultural Context of English Literature*, London: Longman.

Goldthwaite, J. (1996) *The Natural History of Make-Believe: A Guide to the Principal Works of Britain, Europe, and America*, Oxford: Oxford University Press.

Grahame, K. (1980 [1908]) *The Wind in the Willows*, London: Methuen.

Gray, D. (ed.), Carroll, L. (1992) *Alice in Wonderland* 2nd edn, London: W.W. Norton and Company.

—— (1993) *Charlotte's Web: A Pig's Salvation*, New York: Twayne.

Griffiths, J. (1980) '*Charlotte's Web*: a lonely fantasy of love', in F. Butler, *Children's Literature Volume 8*, New Haven and London: Yale University Press.

Griswold, J. (1992) *Audacious Kids: Coming of Age in American Classic Children's Books*, New York: Oxford University Press.

—— (1997) 'The Disappearance of Children's Literature (or Children's Literature as Nostalgia) in the United Sates in the Late Twentieth Century', in S. Beckett (ed.) *Reflections of Change: Children's Literature Since 1945*, Westport, CT: Greenwood Press.

Gruner, E.R. (1998) 'Cinderella, Marie Antoinette, and Sara: roles and role models in *A Little Princess*', *The Lion and the Unicorn*, 22: 163–87.

Hamilton, C. (1933) 'Frater Ave Atque Cale', *The Bookman*, Volume 76: 71–2.

Haviland, V. (1973) *Children and Literature*, London: Bodley Head.

Hawthorn, J. (1996) *Studying the Novel: An Introduction*, 3rd edn, London: Arnold.

Hearn, M.P. (ed.) (1973) *The Annotated Wizard of Oz*, New York: Clarkson N. Potter.

Henty, G.A. (1884) *With Clive In India* or *The Beginnings of an Empire*, London: Blackie & Son.

Hilton, M., Styles, M. and Watson, V. (1997) *Opening the Nursery Door*, London: Routledge.

Hollander, A. (1981) 'Reflections on *Little Women*', *Children's Literature* 9: 28–39.

Hollindale, P. (1988) *Ideology and the Children's Book*, Stroud: Thimble Press.

—— (1999) *Signs of Childness*, Stroud: Thimble Press.

Hunt, J.D. (1982) *The Wider Sea: A Life of John Ruskin*, London: Dent.

—— and Holland, F.M. (1982) *The Ruskin Polygon: Essays on the Imagination of John Ruskin*, Manchester: Manchester University Press.

Hunt, P. (1990) *Children's Literature: The Development of Criticism*, London: Routledge.

—— (1991) *Criticism, Theory and Children's Literature*, Oxford: Blackwell.

—— (ed.) (1992) *Literature for Children: Contemporary Criticism*, London: Routledge.

—— (1994) *An Introduction to Children's Literature*, Oxford: Opus.

—— (ed.) (1995) *An Illustrated History of Children's Literature*, Oxford: Oxford University Press.

—— (ed.) (1998) *Understanding Children's Literature: Key Essays from the 'International Companion Encyclopaedia of Children'*, London: Routledge.

—— (ed.) (2000) *Children's Literature: An Anthology, 1801–1902*, Oxford: Blackwell.

—— (ed.) (2001) *Children's Literature: a Guide*, Oxford: Blackwell.

—— and Lenz, M. (2001) *Alternative Worlds in Fantasy Fiction*, London: Continuum.

Hutcheon, L. (1989) *The Politics of Postmodernism*, London: Routledge.

Jackson, R. (1988) *Fantasy: The Literature of Subversion*, London: Routledge.

Johnston, A. (1959) '*The Water-Babies*: Kingsley's debt to Darwin', *English* 12: 215–9.

Joyce, J. (1972 [1916]) *A Portrait of the Artist as a Young Man*, New York: Viking.

Keyser, E.L. (1983) '"Quite contrary": Frances Hodgson Burnett's *The Secret Garden*', *Children's Literature* 11: 1–13.

Kinghorn, N.D. (1986) 'The real miracle of *Charlotte's Web*', *Children's Literature Association Quarterly* 11: 4–9.

Kingsley, C. (1994 [1863]) *The Water-Babies*, London: Wordsworth.

—— (1995 [1863]) *The Water-Babies*, (ed.) Brian Alderson, Oxford: Oxford World's Classics.

Kingsley, F. (ed.) (1883) *Charles Kingsley: His Letters and Memories of His Life*, New York: Charles Scribner's Sons.

Kipling, R. (1983 [1902]) *The Just So Stories*, London: Macmillan.

Knoepflmacher, U.C. (1998) *Ventures into Childland: Victorians, Fairy Tales and Feminity*, Chicago, IL: University of Chicago Press.

Lawrence, D.H. (1973 [1924]) 'Americans' in *Selected Literary Criticism*, London: Heinemann.

Lawson, V. (1999) *Out of the Sky she Came: The Life of P.L. Travers, Creator of Mary Poppins*, Rydalmere, NSW: Hodder.

Leavis, Q.D. (1976) 'The Water Babies', *Children's Literature in Education* 23: 155–63.

Lecercle, J-J. (1994) *Philosophy of Nonsense: The Intuitions of Victorian Nonsense Literature*, London: Routledge.

Lesnik-Oberstein, K. (1994) *Children's Literature: Criticism and the Fictional Child*, Oxford and New York: Oxford University Press.

—— (ed.) (1998) *Children in Culture: Approaches to Childhood*, London: Macmillan Press.

Levenson, M.H. (1999) *The Cambridge Companion to Modernism*, Cambridge: Cambridge University Press.

Lewis, C.S. (1973) 'On Three Ways of Writing for Children' in V. Haviland, *Children and Literature*, London: Bodley Head.

Lewis, D. (1990) 'Constructedness of texts: picture books and the metafictive', *Signal* 62, May: 131–46.

—— (2001) *Picturing Text: The Contemporary Children's Picturebook*, London: Taylor & Francis Books Ltd.

Littlefield, H.M. (1964) 'The Wizard of Oz: Parable of Populism', *American Quarterly* 16: 47–58.

Locke, J. (1977 [1690]) 'An essay concerning human understanding', *The Locke Reader*, Cambridge: Cambridge University Press.

Lurie, A. (1990) *Don't Tell the Grown-ups: Subversive Children's Literature*, London: Bloomsbury.

MacDonald, G. (1905) 'The Fantastic Imagination', originally published in *A Dish of Orts* (1893), reprinted in *Signal* 16, Jan 1975: 26–32.

—— (1986 [1871]) *At the Back of the North Wind*, New York: Signet.

—— (1990 [1872/1883]) *The Princess and the Goblin/The Princess and Curdie*, Oxford: Oxford University Press.

MacLeod, A.S. (1994) *American Childhood: Essays on Children's Literature of the Nineteenth and Twentieth Centuries*, Georgia: University of Georgia Press.

Mallan, K. (1999) *In the Picture: Perspectives on Picture Books*, Wagga Wagga, NSW: Centre for Information Studies, Charles Sturt University.

Manlove, C.N. (1990) 'MacDonald and Kingsley: a Victorian contrast' in William Raeper (ed.) *The Gold Thread: Essays on George MacDonald*, Edinburgh: Edinburgh University Press.

Manos, N.L. and Rochelson, M.J. (eds) (1994) *Transforming Genres: New Approaches to British Fiction of the 1890s*, New York: St Martin's Press.

May, J. (1997) *Children's Literature and Critical Theory: Reading and Writing for Understanding*, Oxford: Oxford University Press.

McGavran, J.H. Jr (ed.) (1991) *Romanticism and Children's Literature in Nineteenth Century England*, Georgia: University of Georgia Press.

—— (ed.) (1999) *Literature and the Child: Romantic Continuations, Postmodern Contestations*, Iowa City: University of Iowa Press.

McGillis, R. (1996) *The Nimble Reader*, New York: Twayne Publishers.

—— (ed.) (2000) *Voices of the Other: Postcolonial Children's Literature*, New York: Garland.

—— (1996) *A Little Princess: Gender and Empire*, Farmington Hills, MI: Twayne Publishers.

Meek, M. (1988) *How Texts Teach What Readers Learn*, Stroud: Thimble Press.

Meigs, C. *et al.* (1953) *A Critical History of Children's Literature*, New York: Macmillan.

Mellor, A.K. (1993) *Romanticism and Gender*, London: Routledge.

Mills, S. (2000) 'Pig in the middle', *Children's Literature in Education* 31.2: 107–24.

Milne, A.A. (1962 [1917]) *Once on a Time . . .*, London: Edmund Ward, Ltd.

—— (1979 [1928]) *The House at Pooh Corner*, New York: Dell.

—— (1981 [1926]) *Winnie-the-Pooh*, New York: Dell.

Misheff, S. (1998) 'Beneath the web and over the stream: the search for safe places in *Charlotte's Web* and *Bridge to Terabitha*', *Children's Literature in Education* 29: 131–41.

Moi, Toril (1985) *Sexual/Textual Politics*, London: Routledge

Moore, A.C. (1935) 'Mary Poppins', *Horn Book* 11: 6–7.

Moss, A. (1991) 'E. Nesbit's Romantic Child in Modern Dress' in J.H. MacGavran Jr (ed.) *Romanticism and Children's Literature in Nineteenth Century England*, Georgia: University of Georgia Press.

Murray, G. (1998) *American Children's Literature and the Construction of Childhood*, New York: Twayne.

Myers, M. (1992) 'Little Girls Lost: Rewriting Romantic Childhood, Righting Gender and Genre' in G. Sadler (ed.) *Teaching Children's Literature: Issues, Pedagogy, Resources*, New York: MLA.

Nackenoff, C. (1997) 'The Horatio Alger myth' in P. Gerster and N. Cords (eds) *Myth America, Volume II*, New York: Brandywine Press.

Nelson, C. (1989) 'Sex and the single boy: ideals of manliness and sexuality in Victorian literature for boys', *Victorian Studies* 32(4): 525–50.

—— (1994) 'Fantasied de Siècle: Sex and Sexuality in the Late-Victorian Fairy Tale' in N. Manor and M-J. Rochelson (eds) *Transforming Genres New Approaches to British Fiction of the 1890s*, New York: St Martin's Press.

—— (1999) 'Growing Up: Childhood', in H. Tucker, *A Companion to Victorian Literature and Culture*, Oxford: Blackwell.

Nesbit, E. (1973 [1905]) *The Railway Children*, London: Puffin.
—— (1973 [1906]) *The Story of the Amulet*, London: Puffin.
—— (1994 [1906]) *The Railway Children*, London: Puffin.
Nikolajeva, J.M. (1995) *Aspects and Issues in the History of Children's Literature*, Westport, CT: Greenwood Press.
—— (1996) *Children's Literature Comes of Age: Toward a New Aesthetic*, New York: Garland.
—— (2000) *From Mythic to Linear: Time in Children's Literature*, Lanham, MD: Scarecrow Press.
—— and Scott, C. (2001) *How Picture Books Work*, New York: Garland.
Nodelman, P. (1985) *Touchstones: Reflections on the Best of Children's Literature*, Volume one, West Lafayette, IN: Children's Literature Association.
—— (1987) *Touchstones: Reflections on the Best of Children's Literature*, Volume two, West Lafayette, IN: Children's Literature Association.
—— (1988) *Words about Pictures: The Narrative Art of Children's Picture Books*, Athens: University of Georgia Press.
—— (1989) *Touchstones: Reflections on the Best of Children's Literature*, Volume three, West Lafayette, IN: Children's Literature Association.
—— (1992) *The Pleasures of Children's Literature*, White Plains: Longman.
—— (1999) *The Pleasures of Children's Literature* (2nd edn), Harlow: Pearson Professional Education.
Norton, M. (1995 [1952]) *The Borrowers*, London: Puffin.
Nye, R. (1994) 'An Appreciation' in M. Gardner and R. Nye (eds) *The Wizard of Oz and Who He Was*, East Lansing: Michigan State University Press.
Olendorf, Donna (ed.) (1992) *Children's Literature Review Vol 28*, Farmington Hills, MI: The Gale Group.
Otten, C.F. and Schmidt, Gary D. (eds) (1989) *The Voice of the Narrator in Children's Literature: Insights from Writers and Critics*, New York: Greenwood Press.
Parker, D. (1994) 'The rise and fall of *The Wonderful Wizard of Oz* as a "Parable on Populism"', *Journal of the Georgia Association of Historians*, 15: 49–63.
Paul, L. (1987) 'Enigma variations: what feminist criticism knows about children's literature', *Signal* 54 (September): 186–202.
—— (1998) *Reading Otherways*, Stroud: Thimble Press.
Phillips, J. (1993) 'The Mem Sahib, the Worthy, the Rajah and his Minions: some reflections on the class politics of *The Secret Garden*', *The Lion and the Unicorn: A Critical Journal of Children's Literature* 17.2: 168–94.
Phillips, R. (ed.) (1974) *Aspects of Alice*, Harmondsworth: Penguin Books.
Plotz, J. (2001) *Romanticism and the Vocation of Childhood*, New York: Palgrave.
Prickett, S. (1979) 'Adults in allegory land: Kingsley and MacDonald', in *Victorian Fantasy*, Bloomington: Indiana University Press.

—— (1979) *Victorian Fantasy*, Hemel Hempstead: Harvester Press.

Pullman, P. (1994) *The Ruby in the Smoke*, London: Random House.

—— (1997) *Clockwork*, London: Transworld Publishers.

—— (2000) *The Amber Spyglass*, London: Scholastic.

Pykett, L. (ed.) (1996) *Reading Fin de Siècle Fictions*, London: Longman.

Rahn, S. (1985) 'The sources of Ruskin's *Golden River*', *Victorian Newsletter* 68. Fall: 1–9.

Reardon, C. (1996) 'Music as leitmotif in Louisa May Alcott's *Little Women*', *Children's Literature* 24: 74–85.

Reynolds, K. (1990) *Girls Only: Gender and Popular Children's Fiction*, Hemel Hempstead: Harvester/Wheatsheaf.

—— (1994) *Children's Literature of the 1890s and the 1990s*, Plymouth: Northcote House.

Richards, J. (1989) *Imperialism and Juvenile Fiction*, Manchester: Manchester University Press.

Richardson, A. (1984) 'Wordsworth, fairy tales and the politics of children's reading' in G. Summerfield (ed.) *Fantasy and Reason: Children's Literature in the Eighteenth Century*, London: Methuen.

—— (1994) *Literature, Education and Romanticism: Reading as a Social Practice*, Cambridge: Cambridge University Press.

Rollin, L. (1990) 'The reproduction of mothering in *Charlotte's Web*', *Children's Literature* 18: 42–52.

Root, R.L. Jr (ed.) (1994) *Critical Essays on E. B. White*, New York: G. K. Hall.

Rose, J. (1994) *The Case of Peter Pan: or the Impossibility of Children's Fiction*, revised edn, Basingstoke: Macmillan.

Ruland, R. and Bradbury, M. (1991) *From Puritanism to Postmodernism: A History of American Literature*, London: Penguin.

Rushdy, A.H.A. (1991) '"The miracle of the web": community, desire, and narrativity in *Charlotte's Web*', *The Lion and the Unicorn: A Critical Journal of Children's Literature* 15.2: 35–60.

Ruskin, J. (1991 [1856]) *Modern Painters*, vol. I, pt. V.

—— (1978 [1885]) *Praeterita: The Autobiography of John Ruskin*, Oxford: Oxford University Press.

—— (1991) *Selected Writings*, chosen and annotated by K. Clark, London: Penguin Classics.

Scieszka, J. and Smith, L. (1993) *The Stinky Cheese Man*, London: Puffin Books.

Sale, R. (1978) *Fairy Tales and After: from Snow White to E.B. White*, Cambridge, MA: Harvard University Press.

Sandison, A. (ed.) (1987) Rudyard Kipling *Kim*, Oxford: Oxford University Press.

Sendak, M. (1970) *Where the Wild Things Are*, London: Puffin.

Showalter, E. (1991) *Sister's Choice: Tradition and Change in American Women's Writing*, Oxford: Oxford University Press.

—— (1996) 'Syphilis, Sexuality, and the Fiction of the *Fin de siècle,*' in L. Pykett (ed.) *Reading Fin de Siècle Fictions*, London: Longman.

Silver, A.K. (1997) 'Domesticating Bronte's moors: motherhood in the secret garden', *The Lion and the Unicorn: A Critical Journal of Children's Literature* 21.2: 193–203.

Stein, G. (1993 [1939]) *The World is Round*, Boston: Little Barefoot Books.

Stephens, J. (1989) 'Language, discourse, and picture books', *Children's Literature Association Quarterly* 14.3 Fall: 106–10.

Stephens, J. (1992) *Language and Ideology in Children's Literature*, New York: Longmans.

—— (ed.) (1999) *The Classic Fairy Tales: Texts, Criticism*, New York: W.W. Norton.

Stern, M.B. (1996) *Louisa May Alcott*, New York: Random House.

—— (ed.) (1996) *The Feminist Alcott: Stories of a Woman's Power by Louisa M. Alcott*, Boston, MA: Northeastern University Press.

—— (ed.) (1998) *From Blood and Thunder to Hearth and Home*, Boston, MA: Northeastern University Press.

Stevenson, D. (1994) '"If you read this last sentence, it won't tell you anything": postmodernism, self-referentiality and *The Stinky Cheese Man*', *Children's Literature Association Quarterly* 19 (Spring 1994) No. 1: 32–4.

Stone, M. (ed.) (1991) *Children's Literature and Contemporary Theory*, Wollongong: The New Literature Research Centre.

Summerfield, G. (1984) *Fantasy and Reason: Children's Literature in the Eighteenth Century*, London: Methuen.

Tatar, M. (1993) *Off With Their Heads!: Fairy Tales and the Culture of Childhood*, Princeton, NJ: Princeton University Press.

Thacker, D. (1996) *An Examination of Children's Inter-Action with Fiction leading to the Development of Methodologies to Elicit and Communicate Their Responses*, unpublished doctoral thesis.

Thacker, D. (2001) 'Feminine language and the politics of children's literature', *The Lion and the Unicorn*, 25: 3–16.

Thwaite, A. (1974) *Waiting for the party: the life of Frances Hodgson Burnett, 1849–1924*, London: Secker & Warburg.

Townsend, J.R. (1976) *Written for Children*, London: Penguin.

Travers, P.L. (1934) *Mary Poppins*, London: Peter Davies.

—— (1958) *Mary Poppins*, London: Collins.

—— (1967) 'Only connect', *Quarterly Journal of the Library of Congress* 24 October: 238–48.

—— (1968) 'On not writing for children', *Bookbird* 6.4: 3–7.

—— (1982) 'A letter from the Author', *Children's Literature* 10: 214–17.

Tucker, H. (ed.) (1999) *A Companion to Victorian Literature and Culture*, Oxford: Blackwell.

Tucker, N. (1976) *Suitable For Children?*, Brighton: Sussex University Press.
—— (1981) *The Child and the Book*, Cambridge: Cambridge University Press.
Veeser, H.A. (ed.) (1989) *The New Historicism*, New York: Routledge.
—— (ed.) (1994) *The New Historicism Reader*, New York: Routledge.
Wall, B. (1991) *The Narrator's Voice: The Dilemma of Children's Fiction*, London: Macmillan.
Warner, M. (1994) *From the Beast to the Blonde: On Fairy Tales and their Tellers*, London: Chatto & Windus.
Webb, J. (ed.) (2000) *Text, Culture and National Identity in Children's Literature*, Helsinki: Nordinfo.
West, M. (1992) 'The Dorothys of Oz: a heroine's unmaking' in D. Butts (ed.) *Stories in Society*, London: Macmillan.
Wheeler, M. (1985) *English Fiction of the Victorian Period*, London: Longman.
—— (ed.) (1995) *Ruskin and Environment: The Storm-cloud of the Nineteenth Century*, Manchester: Manchester University Press.
White, E.B. (1942) *One Man's Meat*, New York and London: Harper Brothers.
—— (1963 [1953]) *Charlotte's Web*, Harmondsworth: Puffin Books.
Wilde, O. (1992) *The Happy Prince and Other Stories*, London: Puffin.
Wilmer, C. (ed.) (1997) John Ruskin *Unto This Last*, London: Penguin.
Wintle, J. and Fisher, E. (eds) (1974) *The Pied Pipers*, London: Paddington Press.
Wood, N. (1995) 'A (sea) green Victorian: Charles Kingsley and *The Water Babies*', *The Lion and the Unicorn: A Critical Journal of Children's Literature* 19.2: 233–52.
Woolf, V. (1998 [1933]) *Flush*, Oxford: Oxford University Press.
Wordsworth, W. (1936 [1802]) *Poetical Works*, Oxford: Oxford University Press.
—— (1997 [1799]) *The Prelude*, London: Penguin.
Wullschlager, J. (1995) *Inventing Wonderland: The Lives and Fantasies of Lewis Carroll, Edward Lear, J.M. Barrie, Kenneth Grahame and A.A. Milne*, London: Methuen.
Zipes, J. (1983) *Fairy Tales and the Art of Subversion: The Classical Genre for Children and the Process of Civilization*, New York: Wildman.
—— (1989) *Reading Victorian Fairy Tales*, London: Routledge.
—— (ed.) (1992) *Spells of Enchantment: The Wondrous Fairy Tales of Western Culture*, London: Penguin Books.
—— (1999) *When Dreams Come True: Classical Fairy Tales and Their Tradition*, New York: Routledge.

Useful websites

The quality of websites on children's literature is variable for the student and researcher. Those listed below are reliable and provide links to other good sites.

The Children's Literature Association: http://www.ebbs.english.vt.edu.chla
The Children's Literature Web Guide: http://www.acs.ucalgary.ca/~dkbrown/index.html
The National Centre for Research in Children's Literature: http://www.ncrcl.ac.uk/contact.html
Perry Nodelman's site provides a very useful set of bibliographies across a range of areas up until 1995: http://www.uwinnipeg.ca/~nodelman

Journals

Ariel: A Review of International English Literature. Calgary: University of Calgary, launched 1970.
Bookbird – international children's literature: International Board of Books for Youth (IBBY).
Children's Literature Abstracts (CLA): [Birmingham, Eng.]: Sub-section on Library Work with Children of the International Federation of Library Associations, launched 1973.
Children's Literature Association Quarterly (ChLAQ). Winnipeg, Man.: The Association, launched 1988.
Children's Literature in Education (CLE). New York: Agathon Press, launched 1971.
Horn Book Magazine (HB). [Boston, Horn Book] launched 1924.
Lion and Unicorn (L&U). Baltimore, MD: Johns Hopkins UP, launched 1987.
New Review of Children's Literature and Librarianship. (NRCLL). London: Taylor Graham, launched c. 1995.
Orana (Australia). {S.l.}: Library Association of Australia. School & Children's Libraries Sections, 1977.
Papers: Explorations into Children's Literature. Burwood, Australia: Deakin University, launched 1990.
Signal: Approaches to Children's Books. Stroud: Thimble Press, launched 1970.

Index

cultural concerns: British and
American ideas 9; change affecting
definition of childhood 4; gender
divisions in *fin de siècle* period
73–4; recent emphasis on in
literary criticism 5, 6, 8, *see also*
high culture; popular culture
cultural criticism: postmodern 142,
143, 145–6

Darwinian theories 50, 51, 58;
impact on Kingsley 50, 57–8,
58–9, 61–2
David Copperfield (Dickens) 48
Daz4Zoe (Swindell) 145
De Quincey, Thomas 20
deconstruction: in postmodern
children's books 140, 141
Defoe, Daniel: *Robinson Crusoe* 19
detective fiction: Pullman 154
Dickens, Charles 27, 75; concern
over mistreatmment of children
48; *Great Expectations* 51; *The Old
Curiosity Shop* 42
Dickinson, Emily 23, 52
'Disneyfication': of stories 141
Divine Songs (Watts) 20, 21
domestic fiction: for girls 53, 91
Dracula (Stoker) 75
dream: in nineteenth-century
literature 16, 48
Dusinberre, J.: *Alice to the Lighthouse*
2, 106; theory of Modernist art 5

Each, Peach, Pear Plum (Ahlbergs)
158
economy: American expansion and
power 84; interwar hardship in
America 109; Romantic responses
to changes 15, *see also* political
economy
Eden: American idea of creating 33,
51; Burnett's *Secret Garden* 97;
creation of in *The King of the
Golden River* 32; image of in *Alice
in Wonderland* 65, 67–8
education: Carroll's references to in
Alice 64; increased availability of
53; nineteenth-century debates

13–14, 19, 22, 58; Romantic
anxiety about 24; and separation
of children from parents 55
Egoff, S. (*et al*): *Only Connect* 114
Eliot, George: *Middlemarch* 63; *The
Mill on the Floss* 51
Emerson, Ralph Waldo: view of
children 13, 22–3, 51–2
Emile (Rousseau) 19
Eric; or Little by Little (Farrar) 54
Ethel and Ernest A True Story (Briggs)
146
euthanasia: engaged in *Postcards from
No Man's Land* 145
Ewing, Mrs Juliana Horatia 44
existentialism: and *Charlotte's Web*
111, 122–3; as reponse to
Modernist experience 105, 122

Fabian socialism: influence on Nesbit
83
fairy tale 7; Baum's model 85–6, 87;
and *fin de siècle* issues of sexuality
76; influence of translations 8, 15;
Joyce's *Portrait of the Artist* 106–7;
Kingsley's narrative in *The Water-
Babies* 56, 57–8, 59–62;
MacDonald's approach 43;
parodies in *The Stinky Cheese Man*
158–63; playful approach in
Clockwork 148, 152–3, 153–4,
154; postmodern allusions to 143,
148, 157, 163; Romantic support
for 16–18, 18–19, 21, 24, 26–7,
32; Wilde's stories 76–7, 85
family: in *Little Women* 33–4; post-
war changes emphasised in
Norton's work 131
'The Fantastic Imagination'
(MacDonald) 43
fantasy: in Carroll's work 41, 48, 55,
63, 65, 106; and *fin de siècle* issues
of sexuality 76; interaction with
reality in Modernist texts 103,
111, 115, 122–9, 130; Jo's
imaginative world in *Little Women*
37–8; Kingsley 41, 55;
MacDonald's approach 44, 46;
Mary Poppins stories 109, 115,

The Pigman (Zindel) 144–5
Pilgrim's Progress (Bunyan) 61; in
  Little Women 34–5, 37
playfulness: neglect of by cultural
  critics 142; Norton's *The Borrowers*
  133, 134–5; postmodern desire for
  147, 149; Pullman's *Clockwork*
  148, 152–3; and subversion in
  children's books 140, 146, 148
poetry: Dickinson's naive style 52;
  feminine quality of Modernist
  writing 105; Romantic
  contemplations of childhood
  14–15, 21
political economy: relationship with
  morality in *The King of the Golden
  River* 24, 26, 29–30, 32
politics: American tendencies 49;
  and children's books 145–6;
  growth in democracy and
  awareness of rights 15, 45, 84;
  position in *The King of the Golden
  River* 26, 29; Romantic responses
  to revolutionary upheavals 14, 15,
  see also anti-imperialism; anti-
  slavery; Fabian socialism
popular culture: blurring of
  boundaries with the literary
  145–6; tensions with high culture
  84, 85, 139, 146; view of
  children's literature as 7, 73, 85,
  90, 139; and *The Wonderful
  Wizard of Oz* 85, 89
Portrait of the Artist as a Young Man
  (Joyce) 106–7
Postcards from No Man's Land
  (Chambers) 145
postmodernism 2, 5; allusions to
  fairy tales 143, 148, 157, 163;
  anticipation of in later Modernist
  narratives 110–13; challenges to
  dominating master narratives 79,
  110, 139, 140, 141, 142–5,
  148–9, 150; historical roots
  142–3; playful qualities in
  children's books 133–4, 135, 140,
  148; and poststructuralist
  criticism 145–6, 149–50;
  Pullman's *Clockwork* 151–6;

relationship with Modernism 139;
  Romantic model of adult/reader
  relationship 139, 140, 142, 147;
  The Stinky Cheese Man 157–63
poststructuralism 145–6, 149
poverty: effects in urban America 74
power relationships: engaged in
  children's literature 3–4, 8, 81–2,
  112, 139, 141; shifts in *fin de siècle*
  period 73–4
The Prelude (Wordsworth) 18–19
the primitive: Modernist fascination
  with 102, 106, 107
The Princess and Curdie (MacDonald)
  46
The Princess and the Goblin
  (MacDonald) 44, 46, 47
Princess Smartypants (Cole) 143–4
psychoanalytic theory 6, 101, *see also*
  Lacanian psychoanalysis
puberty: awareness of in Cole's
  picture books 144
publishing: nineteenth century 15,
  84; separation of children's market
  109, 110, 112–13
Pullman, Philip 143, 150; *The
  Amber Spyglass* 6–7, 148; *Clockwork*
  148, 151–6; 'His Dark Materials'
  trilogy 148; *The Ruby in the Smoke*
  154
Puritanism: values in *Little Women*
  33, 34

radio: material produced for children
  109
Ragged Dick (Alger) 54
Ransome, Arthur 102; *Swallows and
  Amazons* 109
rationalism: nineteenth-century ideas
  about children 16, 22; nineteenth-
  century subversion of by language
  47, 48; Romantic view of dangers
  of 24; set against fantasy in *Alice
  in Wonderland* 65
readers: blurring of boundaries
  between children and adults
  147–8; growing distance between
  adults and children at turn of
  century 84; postmodern 142, 144,

An environmentally friendly book printed and bound in England by www.printondemand-worldwide.com

PEFC Certified

This product is
from sustainably
managed forests
and controlled
sources

www.pefc.org

PEFC/16-33-415

MIX

Paper from
responsible sources

FSC® C004959

This book is made entirely of chain-of-custody materials; FSC materials for the cover and PEFC materials for the text pages

#0005 - 121112 - C0 - 216/138/11 - PB